Digital Context 2.0

7 Lessons in Business Strategy, Consumer Behavior, and the Internet of Things

David W. Norton, Ph.D.

Gifted Press, LLC.

Gifted Press LLC

9553 Penstemon

Colorado Springs, CO 80920

Websites: gostonemantel.com, thecollaboratives.com

Email: davenorton@gostonemantel.com

Cover Art and Graphics: Tara Kelley-Cruz

ISBN (978-0-9969414-0-2)

ISBN (978-0-9969414-1-9)

Printed in the United States of America

CONTENTS

FOREWORD TO DIGITAL CONTEXT 2.0

The research and ideas in this book will help you focus your business strategy for the wave of digital infusion washing across today's economic landscape. But you will also gain in understanding how they were discovered, shaped, and shared.

I sat in the first meeting of the 2014 Digital Consumer Collaborative, held in Orlando in November of 2013. Representatives from seven companies participated, and even in that first meeting, as we listened to Dave Norton share the early insights that he and the Stone Mantel team uncovered, we began to see consumer decision-making in a new light. As the participants themselves (eventually growing to 14) went out into the field to perform their own ethnographic studies and brought back their findings, the subject slowly came into focus. And now, through dialogue, research, and framework development, it's clear that the Collaborative gained incomparable insight into how people interact digitally, and moreover how companies can generate economic value by catering to their individual needs.

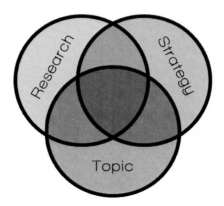

The Digital Consumer Collaborative is a blend of research, strategy, and discussion focused on a set of forward-looking topics that unfolds over a year. Using a design-thinking methodology called the Mantel Method, we work together, go deep into the lives of consumers, and build concepts that benefit all of the companies involved. Each year the members of the Collaborative write a charter that focuses on the next two- to three-year horizon. And the goal of the work is to help the companies involved design strategies *before* they are caught in the crosshairs of digital disruption.

Who else is doing this sort of collaboration? Not South by Southwest or other such conferences. The big name research and analytic houses? Not the same; this is boutique. Who else is bringing companies together to innovate for the benefit of all, using the best practices of design thinking? No one that I can think of.

The Digital Consumer Collaborative is research as a transformative experience for all participants. It's strategy creation as a collaborative experience. It's about going deep and working alongside smart people from other companies and disciplines. Any company could benefit from this type of collaboration because of the value that comes from dialogue, debate, and interdisciplinary thinking.

And the value created by this Collaborative has been extensive, as you will see from reading this book. There's a lot of conjecture about what will happen because of the onslaught of technology and the Internet of Things in particular. The arguments that Dave Norton presents here in *Digital Context 2.0* on behalf of the Collaborative are compelling and insightful because the concepts have been vetted and based on the direct observation of consumers.

As Dave makes clear, businesses that hope to gain access to consumers in today's digitally-infused world must not only understand and embrace but access the context of individual, living, breathing customers. (And oh, by the way, as the consumerization of technology continues apace this all applies to business users as well). Companies must go beyond omni-channels to embed themselves into the lives of customers, anticipating the jobs they want done in order to "close the gap between a consumer's thoughts and actions" as Dave puts it. Through the Internet of Things, businesses must already be there in the customer's mind, heart, and digital device. Always there, at the ready, waiting to spring into action lest the opportunity to impact that customer's life disappears.

Dave guides us through the conversations that most companies are dealing with internally today. Chapter 1 focuses on how wearables change the way we think about the jobs customers hire us to do and consequently the business models we create to produce economic value. Chapter 2 goes deep into consumer behavior and channel strategy. Omni-channel is not a stopping point. It's a precursor to Digital Context. Chapter 3 presents the findings from a recent quantitative study designed to gauge consumer receptivity to the Internet of Things. It turns out, there's a lot of consumers that are already ready in the here and now. Chapter 4 argues for the radical idea of a whole new approach to customer segmentation and value proposition design based on the "mode" a consumer is in. Chapter 5 takes on data, permission, and experience design, while Chapter 6 argues that for Digital Context outdated loyalty paradigms become traps and presents a new framework for producing customer happiness. And Chapter 7 provides a case example that pulls all of the concepts together. Each chapter relates to the others but could also be the basis for a whole book itself. Its very structure forces you to think outside of your set of roles and responsibilities and embrace the fundamental ways your business creates value.

I suggest you read this book from start to end. And then read it from end back to the beginning to fully understand its lessons.

I remember first working with Dave back in 1999 shortly after my book came out, *The Experience Economy: Work Is Theatre & Every Business a Stage* (co-authored with my partner at Strategic Horizons, Jim Gilmore). Dave, whip-smart as he is, immediately recognized the value that the concepts of the Experience Economy could provide companies.

And so we began a collaboration that has lasted over fifteen years now, through the creation of his own firm, insights consultancy Stone

Mantel, in which Dave eventually asked me to partner. Throughout our work together, Dave's unassuming manner belied a brilliant mind. The Mantel Method he developed has helped our wide array of clients solve the most vexing of business challenges. And what I love most about Dave and the growing team at Stone Mantel is that every client engagement yields new frameworks, models that described what the client was facing and prescribed what to do about it. The Digital Consumer Collaborative that Stone Mantel has facilitated over the past two years is no exception.

The advantages of learning from its work and taking action now are huge. Never before have so many "dumb" things become smart. The transformation outlined here in *Digital Context* will impact your customer interactions and economic offerings in profound and unforeseen ways. It all starts by gaining insights from being "in queue." That's the job you need to get done now by reading this book.

But the work of understanding consumers is never done. The research goes on. Perhaps when you finish reading, you too will want to collaborate with us.

B. Joseph Pine II
Co-author, *The Experience Economy*,
Infinite Possibility, and *Authenticity*
Strategic Thought Leader, Stone Mantel

CHAPTER ONE

A WATCH IS NOT A WATCH

Business Models in the Age of the Contextual Home

Lesson 1

A watch that is wearable is not a watch in the world of the Internet of Things (IoT). An IoT-enabled razor is not a razor. An Iot-enabled hearing aid is not a hearing aid. In the IoT world the consumer hires the tool to do much more than what you originally intended the product to do. They can each do the basic functionality that their names imply, but they do much more and will be hired by consumers to do more than what the name of the item suggests – perhaps much more. This shift in purpose affects all aspects of a company's business model.

It's Not a Watch

Samsung could see it coming. In the fall of 2013, Samsung rushed to market a smart watch, the Galaxy Gear. At the time, Acer, Apple, BlackBerry, Foxconn/Hon Hai, Google, LG, Microsoft, Qualcomm, Sony, and Toshiba were also designing watches. Garmin, Polar, and Soleus had GPS watches on the market. Samsung wanted to be the first smart watch designed as a wearable, and certainly wanted to beat Apple to the punch. They beat Apple by almost eighteen months. In the meantime most of the other providers of wrist watch wearables had pulled back. Consumers were not buying smart watches the way they bought smart phones. The prevailing question was: what's the purpose of having a smart watch? Especially when you have a smart phone with so much more functionality.

Still, on April 24, 2015 Apple started shipping the Apple Watch. The initial launch was limited, by Apple standards. In the first three months, 2.9 million watches were sold in the U.S., a tidy number for the big guys. Samsung by comparison had sold/shipped a mere 1.4 million over the previous 18 months. Clearly Apple was doing it again. But doing what? What is the Apple Watch for? Why would a company that has driven so much innovation in digital care about a smarter device to wear on your wrist that tells time? They are not.

The Apple Watch is not a watch but rather a tracking device. It's an alert system and it's part of a growing ecosystem of devices that are connected to each other. But it is not a watch any more than an iPhone is a telephone. The conventional name does not imply the primary purpose of the wearable. At the same time, consumers are not buying Apple Watches because they want a more accurate timepiece. What they *do* want are tools that track their biofeedback and help them to improve their health and wellbeing. They want a tool that alerts them about important things that they should be paying attention to. They want a device that is connected to their phone, tablet, computer, DVR, gaming system, home security network, and can also be used as a camera. As with the iPad, most consumers believe that version 1.0 of Apple Watch is good, but 2.0 will open up a whole new range of possibilities, as will successive iterations after that.

It is that world of new possibilities that this book is focused on. Robert Scoble and Shel Israel in *Age of Context: Mobile, Sensors, Data and the Future of Privacy*, describe the world of the Internet of Things, of mobility and data as a world of 'context' in which networks of tools and environments work together to enhance our lives. Basically, the Internet of Things (IoT) is the network of physical objects from appliances to shelves and cabinets to walls, windows and doors (to name a few possibilities). They contain embedded sensory technology, both wired and wireless, through which they communicate and interact with each other to create a smart or intelligent environment (known in some circles as "Ambient Intelligence or AmI) to better serve the needs and desires of the users of that environment. This is a concept that will rapidly become a reality. As

Vermesan, Freiss (and others, 2014) point out, "The number of Internet-connected devices surpassed the number of human beings on the planet in 2011, and by 2020, Internet-connected devices are expected to number between 26 billion and 50 billion."
Source: http://www.internet-of-things-research.eu/pdf/IERC_Cluster_Book_2014_Ch.3_ SRIA_WEB.pdf

If you have used Google Now, you have already experienced the digital 'context' that Scoble and Israel describe, and which is a major focus of this book. You understand how data from multiple tools on your Android device are brought together to assist you, whether it be to ensure you leave for an appointment on time, or remember an important anniversary. Using location, calendar, and weather data, Google Now can suggest that you pack an umbrella for your trip and so much more. Google Now is only one example of a wide spectrum of innovations that are coming. These innovations will empower people to act and create a cocoon of data around their lives. Digital Context, the new business imperative, has as much potential to change consumer behavior and business models as mobility did. (While a fuller description is presented later in this chapter, Digital Context briefly defined is an integrated set of digital tools and environments that anticipate, curate, and connect things for the consumer, and close the gap between a person's thoughts and actions). Companies who understand how to leverage the IoT, wearables, data, and environments will have an advantage over their competitors commensurate with the advantage that app developers (the ones who got it right) had when the smart phone took off. And that's why Apple introduced the Apple Watch.

For the past two years, a small group of individuals from fourteen companies have worked together to study the direction of digital consumer behavior, develop concepts to understand Digital Context, and collaborated to develop actionable insights that will guide their companies toward successful strategies in this fast emerging world. Me and my colleagues at Stone Mantel, have led this initiative called the Digital Consumer Collaborative. This book represents my point of view on how business strategy and tactics should evolve to meet the technologies we are already using in our homes, our cars, the stores we frequent, and to get to the places we travel. My perspective is based on hundreds of hours of in-depth interviews with digital consumers over the last few years, two major quantitative studies, and working sessions with the very smart members of the Digital Consumer Collaborative. I am only sharing with you a portion of the research and findings we've gathered. These insights are general in nature and apply across industries. Each of the companies that participated has collected or received very specific research into their customers' lives as well. Our findings pertain to every aspect of consumer behavior and impact every part of business models that pertain to digital. So let's jump right in.

The Home is the Digital Hub

To illustrate the potential impact of Digital Context on our lives, consider the home for a moment. The basics of modern living have not changed since the introduction of indoor plumbing. Most homes today have pretty much the same wall structure, electrical systems, HVAC, door locks, and electrical appliance types that existed in homes thirty-years ago. Indoor plumbing, of course, came into being well before that, yet I'm being only partly facetious, because you get my point: we build homes pretty much the same way we always have. They are, for the most part, dumb environments—and I'll explain more what I mean by 'dumb' in a moment.

Yet, for most consumers, a home is just not a home without "populating" it with some pretty sophisticated, though mostly discrete technology. Our TVs, internet-connected desktop computers, tablets, laptops, gaming systems, DVRs, printers/scanners/copiers are all a normal part of our lives. Each year these technologies get smarter. And each year more appliances, home networks, and devices come into our homes, each more sophisticated, each with more features than its predecessor. While cars are likely to become the first fully automated environments to support Digital Context, contextual homes will have the greatest impact on both consumers and the companies they buy from.

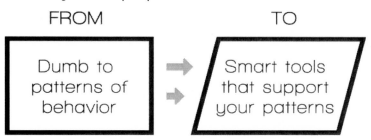

The home is the digital hub of consumers' lives. It is where we go to unwind, to connect with family, to make memories, and to raise our children. Within the walls of our homes, we play out patterns of living. The way you clean your house may not be the way I clean mine. We might have different preferences for dinnertime and things we like to eat. But within every room from kitchen, to family den, to bedroom to bath, and within every type of convenience from refrigerator, to stove, to washers and dryers, and air conditions, even to the very types of flooring you prefer, there are patterns of living. The walls of most homes today are 'dumb' to these patterns. Your current house cannot suggest a cleaning regimen to you even though your life follows similar routines. But if your mop could communicate with your phone or your laptop, it might be able to recommend certain things to you to make your life easier. As I write this an article appears on the front page of the *Wall Street Journal*. "Google unveils OneHub, a smart wifi router," the headline says. The article describes an upgraded home network router that integrates with your home. Let me just quote a little from the article, dated August 18, 2015:

> *Google entered a new business Tuesday, revealing a $200 app-controlled Wi-Fi router capable of managing many aspects of our increasingly complex home networks. It intelligently seeks ways to reduce Wi-Fi congestion, and lets you allocate bandwidth to devices that need it most, like your Netflix-streaming Roku or Apple TV. It can diagnose connection problems, distinguishing between what's happening on your home network and what might be happening with your service provider. It can identify all the devices on your network, and keeps things locked down with a password that's strong but easy to share to trusted people via an app.*
>
> *And while it has the latest flavor of Wi-Fi (AC) and a 360-degree antenna array for pointing the Wi-Fi in your direction, wherever you are, its specs also include two other forms of wireless—Bluetooth and ZigBee (aka 802.15.4)—which enable the router to talk to smart-home appliances. Google doesn't specifically say what these would do, instead labeling them as "future friendly." One thing is clear; this combination of wireless protocols will allow the device to use Weave, a new Google communication system for connected devices to talk to each other using a common language.*

Google is building the infrastructure to manage your home. The promise of Digital Context for your home comes in functional, emotional, social and aspirational forms. You can secure your home and access it remotely. You can track maintenance of HVAC systems or passively monitor the integrity of the pipe system itself. Command your environment to perform based on your mood, setting lighting, temperature, and so forth. Or be able to access information about family members that will benefit their heath or wellbeing. Set goals for yourself and your family and watch as the in-home devices help you accomplish those goals. Everything from apparel to toothbrushes could be connected to the Internet of Things. Turn on a light, there is data that is collected. Open your fridge and take out a beverage, there is more data. Through this interconnectivity of devices, very detailed patterns of a consumer's life can be established.

Efforts are already underway not only to collect such information, but to use it to design an active, communicative interconnectivity into the monitoring devices and sensors from which the information is sourced. Google Nest, for example, creates a connective network through which its products communicate directly with each other. Thus when the Nest Thermostat is set to "Away," the Nest Cam automatically switches to "On" for security monitoring. However the vision is to have many other devices connect with it, such that your smart wristband, which monitors your sleep, can tell your thermostat that you have awakened early and 'please turn up the heat' in wintertime; or your smart car that relay information about the time you are estimated to arrive home, and ask Nest Thermostat to 'please turn up the air conditioning' in summertime. Even further, technology incorporated into the future construction of homes and apartments (through both wired and wireless sensors built into walls and ceilings) may not only allow the same information (e.g., that you just got out of bed a little early) to be transmitted, thus eliminating the need to wear your smart wristband, but such systems will actually be able to "learn" your typical sleeping and waking habits and adjust environmental conditions accordingly, or simply to start the coffee machine brewing in the kitchen so that it ready by the time you get there.
Source: http://www.forbes.com/sites/bernardmarr/2015/08/05/
googles-nest-big-data-and-the-internet-of-things-in-the-connected-home/2/

With respect to personal health, Vitality.net is currently running clinical trials of a Talking Pill Bottle. Called GlowCap and designed to fit most standard pharmacy pill bottles, the cap reminds the patient/consumer to take their prescribed medications, and it can also share information with the patient's doctors, as well as order refills in timely fashion. Taking this a step further, a smart medicine cabinet may someday be able, not only to remind the patient to take his or her medications, but to alert loved ones and health care providers when those medications have not been taken on time or as prescribed. That's a feature that could be extremely valuable when you consider the aging population of baby boomers who fiercely wish to remain independent and will inevitably find themselves living alone.

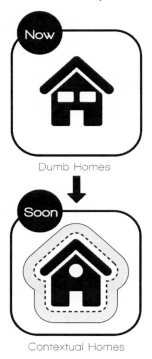

Just think about how many things there are in your home that could be connected to the Internet of Things:

- Doors, windows, cupboards, drawers, closets, and shelves
- Floors
- Outlets, lighting, wiring, faucets, plumbing, HVAC, and thermostats
- Shirts, pants, socks, shoes, underwear, blankets, pillows
- Sports equipment, toys, balls, bicycles
- Tool boxes, hammers, drills, ratchet sets
- Sound equipment, door bells, and alarms

- Razors, shaving cream packaging, soap dishes, lotions, hair dryers, and all other bathroom items
- Food packaging, dishes, cooking utensils, mixers, microwaves, fridges, and dishwashers
- Plants, decorations, pictures, and memorable items
- Irons, fresheners, washers and dryers, and laundry baskets

And these are just the things that make up your daily life. Think about how your life would be affected by the following:

- If your home were enabled to support your medical needs. From the dispensing of pills to the monitoring of glucose, devices you already use should be able to talk to each other and support you
- If you could manage your home for greatest financial benefit and risk reduction. Think about monitors to reduce wasteful uses of energy and data collection that tracks your spending patterns on food, which then makes recommendations on what produce to buy based on supermarket availability, data that the system also tracks. It could happen

To the last point, Greg Geib, a research strategist with American Family Insurance and a member of the Digital Consumer Collaborative said recently, "We have to push our thinking around the role of data in consumers' lives and how we all can benefit from being a part of the same ecosystem." If a watch is not a watch, then in a contextual world, insurance is more than just the insurance…Greg gets that.

Notice that I left off of the list the things that are almost certainly already in your home and connected to the Internet (which indeed, would be far less useful and versatile if they were *not* connected to it): gaming systems, tablets, TVs, computers, and of course, the brains of it all, your smartphone. Skeptics within your company will say that there are a lot of things that could be monitored by sensors that shouldn't be. The consumer doesn't want it, they will say. There will be others within your organization who will see this new technology as a beautiful blue space opportunity.

"What we could do with that data!?" these others will exclaim. Which side speaks the truth? To be sure, there are caveats to bear in mind. Consumers will only want a contextual home (or store, or car, or hotel) if the tools within the environment help them to close the gap between thought and action. You can't just put sensors in things and expect consumers to be wowed. You also can't just be intrusive or disruptive to people's lives. It has to help get a job done. And the data? There needs to be a purpose for collecting data; and permission given, and the ability to deliver on your promise; otherwise you're not in.

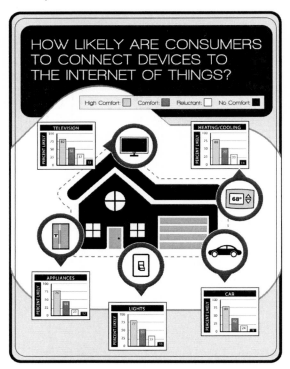

Amazon is currently beta testing a program that illustrates the opportunity that Digital Context represents. Called Dash, the program provides buttons that can be attached to almost any consumer good in your home. Tide, Bounty, Clorox, Gatorade, Kraft Mac & Cheese—you can order any button delivered to your home. Place the button next to your bottle of Tide and as soon as you run out just push the button. The next day Tide arrives at your doorstep. The program is new so at this point, Amazon is still very much testing the waters. But if you are a discount retail supercenter, you have to be wondering what Dash might mean for your business. And if you're a consumer goods company, then you are likely wondering (or you should be) if *you* could pull off resale/replenishment activity by yourself. Do you really need Amazon if you put the sensor that triggers the reorder right in your packaging?

When you have a button that replenishes supply at the point of use, you have a powerful means of disrupting your own channel. Suddenly those who provide the solution become the retailing platform owners. More to the point, repurchase data tells you about the patterns of the home. You may very well not want Amazon to own that data, unless they are willing to share it with you. Amazon may then decide that owning the home environment is more important than charging for certain products. In a battle to own the point of use, companies may find themselves giving product away to own the most valuable retail real estate ever: the kitchen or pantry, the living room, or the laundry room; we don't yet know.

We do know that the home will change—as will every other environment. The following are just a few of the changes that will occur in the home and other places.

1. Consumers will manage a greater number of queues. As the number of alerts, content, apps, networks, and solutions increase, so will the number queues. Consumers will both turn on and turn off queues. Queues will become the primary channels for engaging consumers.

2. In order to maximize their effectiveness and enjoyment, consumers will spend more time 'in mode.' They will expect context-aware environments to help them 'get into a mode.' For companies, understanding modes will become a key component of value proposition design, replacing target demographics as the primary means of understanding what the target audience wants or needs.

3. Because so much activity about consumer's lives will be embedded in the tools and environments that consumers use and engage, the way the customer journeys through experiences will change. In most homes already today consumers often use their digital tools to do multiple things at the same time. They watch TV *while* they shop online. They prepare dinner *while* they post to Facebook. Customer journey mapping will need to focus less on key moments and more on the power of while.

4. Consumers will want things to talk to each other. The power of Digital Context comes from more things that share data with each other. Although security and privacy are serious concerns, over time consumers will become increasingly comfortable with the fact that the products they buy share data with other products—if it means that they are more able to get jobs done that they want to get done.

5. Everything becomes a tool. Digital has the effect on products of turning everything into a tool. Media channels become tools. Travel bags with sensors become tools. If it's smart, it functions like a tool. Positioning a smart product must focus on the functional, emotional, social, and aspirational jobs consumers want to get done.

Think of it this way. When you take everyday, ordinary household objects like shaving razors, mops, macaroni boxes and Gatorade bottles, as well as the very shelves inside refrigerators and medicine cabinets, and embed them with the technology to communicate with the digital devices already in your home, those objects and shelves in effect become sensors themselves. They can track usage data, signal replenishment needs automatically, perhaps even someday suggest product alternatives or efficiencies based on the data they collect.

Over the course of our research in studying the effects of digital on consumer's lives and the impact of context on people's lives, we've adopted specific terminology to describe the concepts as we understand them. Let me share a few of those terms now.

- A tool: A tool is any device or software that is smart and helps the user get things done. Apps, websites, cloud capabilities, and software are tools. So are routers, wearables, smart phones, laptops, smart thermostats, etc. If it has data that it uses to help you accomplish a goal, it's a tool

- An environment: An environment is a place that sensors or other devices effectively connect to the Internet of Things and turn the place into a 'smart' place. Your home, car, or favorite vacation rental could each be an environment. Stores, bank branches, cities, parking lots, and sports arenas are also potential environments. Consumers expect the smarts of the environment to support the activities that naturally occur within that environment, whether those are the sort of activities that might be regarded as "traditional" to that environment, or newer ones made possible by smart tools and the smart environment itself. A technology environment—like the integrated platforms of Apple or Microsoft solutions—is a different, very important part of the equation. To distinguish it from physical environments, we almost always refer to a technology environment, the integrated software services of companies, as a platform

Consumers primarily interact *with* tools *in* environments. While platform-driven tools can by themselves create context, the real magic comes when environments and tools work together.

- *The Internet of Things*, or IoT (sometimes called the Internet of Everything or Ambient Intelligence), refers to a proposed development of the Internet in which everyday objects have network connectivity, allowing them to send and receive data, and network responsiveness, allowing these systems to initiate actions based on that received information. A company like Google or Apple could create proprietary platforms for connected things that would not necessarily be a part of IoT, but would serve the same purpose

- *Digital Context*, which could be shortened to 'context' if there is understanding regarding the meaning, refers to the wide range of innovations that will empower people to act and create a cocoon of data around their lives. Digital Context is an integrated, smart group of channels that close the gap between a consumer's thoughts and actions. Whereas omni-channel strategy focuses on creating a seamless experience for consumers regardless of channel, Digital Context strategy focuses on anticipating needs of consumers by drawing upon clues from different data sources to describe in the moment what the consumer is likely to want or need

- A *queue* is an interface between the consumer and tools that allows the consumer to think quickly and act fast, or to meander, put things on hold, sort and consume content, and be alerted in a timely fashion. Every major online brand today queues things for consumers: Pandora, Facebook, Netflix, Amazon, Google Search, and Uber to name a few. And consumers have become very use to the idea that their interactions with technology will include things like tabs, streams, pinned items, app folders, shopping carts, and inboxes—all of which are queues

- A *mode* is a mindset and a pattern of behavior that a consumer 'gets into' in order to be most effective and derive the most productivity or enjoyment (or a number of other modal functionalities) from a digital experience. While each consumer has his or her own unique way of doing things, there are general observable patterns of activity that companies can focus on and name as a mode to target. In the world of micro moments that make up today's digital activity, modes are a primary attribute of a great value proposition and companies should target them. A participant in one of our Digital Ethnography studies described her experience of "getting into mode" this way in her journal:

"Being productive has a lot to do with the tools I have access to. If I have limitless functionality I can create, organize, produce, etc., for hours. My environment plays a role as well. I will be more productive in a quiet work environment, whereas being around music and friends switches me to playing, socializing mode (happy mood). Technology not only supports my modes/ moods, it is instrumental. For example, I just recently became a tablet owner (yes, I'm very late) and I have found myself to be incredibly productive ever since (using productivity content such as Evernote, Numbers, Pages, Keynote, etc.). As far as technology supporting my happy mood... social media, movies, music, being able to watch a hockey game on my phone when I'm not at home! Are you kidding me? Technology is key to my happiness."

- A *job to get done* is a need or want that a consumer has and is willing to hire a company to deliver or fulfill on. Most jobs to get done have functional, emotional, social, and aspirational dimensions to them. The experience that a company creates for its customers needs to get the right job done for customers. Functional, emotional, social, and aspirational activities often conform to a job archetype. A product that primarily helps you to accomplish a task conforms to a functional archetype. A product that primarily helps you to feel deeply about a moment employs an emotional archetype. A social archetype helps consumers to relate to others. An aspirational archetype focuses on helping consumers to change something about themselves. Each archetype sets expectations for a type of engagement and happiness from the experience

Because of the increasing numbers of tools and the transformation of locations into environments, a company's product is likely to take the form of a set of solutions that are connected to themselves and to other solutions through Application Program Interfaces (APIs) and data exchange. The competition will also sit within similar or the same network. You can

imagine that a highly connected home becomes both a place to support the consumer as well as a place to compete for the consumer's loyalty. The same would be true for the car, store, or any other location. This may well entail the need to radically change your business model, or at minimum to significantly re-evaluate the model's focus. For example, in July of 2015, the Washington Post reported that of the 2.1 million subscribers that AT&T added to its cellular network over the preceding three months, nearly 63 percent of those new connections came from internet-enabled cars. The upshot, AT&T's strongest growth apparently isn't coming from cellphone service anymore.
Source: https://www.washingtonpost.com/news/the-switch/wp/2015/07/23/atts-strongest-growth-isnt-coming-from-cellphone-service-its-in-cars/

Companies need to see their presence within Digital Context as a field of play. They need to understand how the dynamics of environments and tools work together to support the consumer, what opportunities exist across tools or because of different permissions you have for collection, analysis, and usage of data, and within certain queues (a topic I will discuss in more detail in chapter 5). This understanding that you are a player within a dynamic field of opportunity and competition is essential to business strategy today. Mobility already creates a field of play through the range of app tools and device connectivity that occurs. The seamless experience that so many companies want to produce through their omni-channel efforts further enhances the dynamic nature of strategy. These things already exist and Digital Context will only amplify them. To gain advantage within a field of play you must know:

- How to engage consumers through queues
- How to target the modes consumers will want to be in when they are engaged with your company
- How to develop tools that work with other tools and environments
- How to leverage different data types
- How to gain advantage through leveraging recurring jobs to get done

I would also add to this list how to build a business model that is durable and yet addresses the ever-changing field play. The number of new entrants into the field of play will continue to grow. The incumbents will work to own the field. Mapping the consumer's life will be an ongoing effort that won't stand still.

Consumers hire the job; not the business model

Mobile caught so many companies by surprise but Digital Context shouldn't. Mobility and online shopping disrupted their businesses and they could not adjust their business models fast enough to react. It is a mistake to assume that Digital Context will lead to success for every business. Harvard professor Clayton Christensen, an oft-cited authority on innovation and business strategy, constantly reminds us that consumers hire the job to get done. May I suggest an additional adage?

People don't hire business models; they hire jobs to get done.

> People don't hire
> business models; they
> hire jobs to get done.

Consumers hire solutions that help them do functional, emotional, social, and aspirational jobs, and they do not, frankly, care about the business models behind the company's solution. They certainly don't care about channels. In many cases, the channel was originally designed to control the consumer's ability to get the job done in a way that was profitable to the company. If you wanted to secure something to a wall, you had to go to your local hardware store and choose from a limited selection of 'hole-in-the-wall' solutions. The store likely carried a selection of hammers, nails, a few nail guns, some drills, screws, and maybe an auger. By limiting selection and recommending solutions the delivery channel narrowed the pipeline of possibilities and helped maintain price. Digital doesn't just vastly increase selection or level pricing, it fundamentally changes the nature of what a channel is. There is often little or no separation between how a message or a capability is delivered and how the message or capability is used. For example, apps are both delivery and usage tools.

People hire the job to get it done and they often don't really care about the hammer, just the solution. People don't care about your ability to segment them. They don't care about your ability to write a value proposition. They only care about your customer relations strategy if it advantages them *and* helps them get the job done. They certainly don't care about your cost structure. If everything could be free and do a good job they'd be quite happy. You wouldn't be, but they would. It's not because consumers are bad people, right? It's just the nature of the game. They are hiring you to get the job done and if they can accomplish that digitally and for little or no money and in little or no time, they will do that every time.

Some of the most important innovations in business modeling of the last twenty-years are likely to evolve once again because of Digital Context.

The Impact of Digital Context on Business Models

There's a great primer on models written by Osterwalder and Pigneur, called *Business Model Generation.* The fundamental guiding principle of a business model, as they put it, is to "describe the rationale of how an organization creates, delivers and captures value." The components of a business model are interlocking pieces that work together, from customer segments and value propositions to cost structure and revenue streams. Its durability is predicated on the notion that the model represents a sound, viable mechanism for attracting and engaging customers, but also on the calculation that it is scalable, meaning that it offers the potential for positive economic growth of the company. However, the durability of the business model depends in large part on the durability of the channel or channels it relies on to attract and keep a steady stream of loyal customers, or its ability to adapt its channel strategy as those channels evolve and change.

Changes to channels affect resources, customer segmentation, revenue streams, costs, technologies, the customer journey, and so on.

They affect the key activities performed on a daily basis by managers and employees as well as the key business partnerships the company engages in. Without a solid business model a company cannot realize value from solutions they create. And without an understanding of where channels are headed no business model can survive.

But the way companies create business models has not kept up with the times. To build your new business model you likely need to regroup around new types of jobs to get done. As consumers interface with queues and use digital tools, your approach to business modeling will need to become more dynamic. It used to be that a company could do jobs for customers, charge a fee, and then through incremental improvement over time improve the product, thus retaining continued or ongoing sales through maintaining customer loyalty, and even finding innovative ways to get customers to pay for some of those incremental improvements or upgrades. In today's world, you need a forward-looking lens to apply to every aspect of business model design. As a group of cross-industry practitioners and innovation leaders, the Digital Consumer Collaborative has touched on every aspect of business model design. In the rest of this book I will discuss our findings related to:

1. Customer Segments

Most companies define their customer segments using demographic and psychographic data. These techniques were developed decades before the advent of digital mobility. Companies that expect digital to play a major role in their business strategy (that would be all companies, virtually) would benefit from using segmentation techniques that focus specifically on patterns in consumer behavior first and then demographics or psychographics. Our research shows that consumers can and often should be profiled and targeted based on the 'mode' that they are in. A 'mode' is both a pattern of behavior and a mindset, and data can be collected to help companies focus more critically on modes. As we will see in this book, consumer more and more will *want* companies to be aware of and focused on the modes they are in.

2. Customer Journey

Customer journey design is a powerful business model element. It strengthens value propositions, clarifies customer segments, and helps companies align key activities, channels, and resources. Customer journey design has primarily focused on key moments and moments of truth. Digital changes the nature of decision-making, allowing the consumer to meander much more and make decisions while doing other things, or even to freeze decisions indefinitely. Because channels converge and tools and environments talk to each other, customer journey design should include modes, milestones, tools, reminders, and environments. Journey work that is episodic and linear is likely to lead to the wrong kinds of business models for the future.

3. Value Propositions

Value propositions can include attributes such as newness, performance, customization, design, brand/status, price, cost reduction, risk reduction, accessibility, and convenience, but the most important part of your value proposition is the promise you make regarding the job or jobs to get done. Value proposition design must become hyper-focused on jobs to get done because digital is a world of tasks to get done, apps to accomplish things, and multitasking. As I will describe in detail, companies should prioritize jobs that are recurring, or can be made so. If a job need only be done occasionally, it probably will not yield the on-going, dynamic relationship most consumer-facing companies seek to have with their customers. Digital can quickly level the playing field around all other proposition attributes (newness, design, price, etc.), and possibly make some of them irrelevant. When you focus on jobs and you target modes you are much more likely to build a value proposition that will endure technological shifts.

4. Channels

Most companies realize today that they need an omni-channel strategy, even if functionally they are still performing as a multi-channel brand. The advent of the *Internet of Things* and the ability to share data between tools means that channel strategy will continue to evolve toward Digital Context. This is important, especially for retail environments who are seeking to differentiate themselves from pure online retail plays. As mentioned, when a channel becomes smart it queues things and becomes both a tool and a queue. Queues, whether for content, sales, delivery/usage, retail, or customer service, are fundamentally different from traditional channels. They are the most effective way for a consumer and a device to interact. Channels that do not become queues disappear. Queuing is both a feature of technology and a behavior of consumers. They sort, they organize, and they try to anticipate. Any company that doesn't design with queues in mind will likely compete against a solution that does; and the competition will win.

5. Customer Relationship

Building relationships has always required an understanding of who people are and what they want. Faced with digital disruption, many companies doubled down on customer service as a way of maintaining customer relationships. Yet consumers often choose the simplicity and immediacy of digital over any perceived "intimacy" of personal assistance. Digital Context creates a concierge experience that is very different from traditional personal assistance, dedicated assistance, or self-service, and companies are going to need to create a very different approach to customer relationships. As technology becomes more embedded into our lives—whether it's in our homes or on (or literally in) our bodies, the responsibility that companies have for the well-being of consumers increases. Companies should shift from focusing on loyalty to focusing on positive engagement, which we explore in chapter 6.

6. Revenue Streams

A sound business model must make money. Revenue streams are critical to digital strategy. They are also difficult to establish. Because it aligns with queuing, subscription has become the dominant revenue model of digital business. Companies struggle to find ways to get consumers to pay for subscriptions when other products offer similar solutions for free. That may always be the case going forward. But there are things you can do to generate revenue. When you create differentiated content and innovation that supports recurring jobs that consumers value, you have more opportunity to charge them for it. When you leverage your 'field of play' you will often find more revenue for your organization. (See more in Key Activities).

7. Key Resources

Traditionally, companies have defined their key resources as things that are physical, financial, intellectual, or human. They should add to their key resources shared data. Companies protect and produce key resources. Data from consumers is a critical shared resource that makes the world of Digital Context possible and helps consumers close the gap between thinking and doing. Companies who produce content should see the combination of data and content, which I am calling **The Package**, as a primary key resource. Used properly, data shared by consumers enhances physical, financial, intellectual, and human resources.

8. Key Activities

Strengths and capabilities in production, problem solving, and technology platforms, the primary types of key activities in most business models, have been dramatically impacted by digital activity. (Just think about the cloud). As more tools connect to the Internet of Things and as consumers engage with companies through more queues, a key activity is understanding and capitalizing on their strategic field of play. The field of play is the strategic environment of data, tools, environments, queues, and products that companies can or should affect. The field of play often creates parameters for the company's digital strategy. Companies can create competitive advantages through digital by finding leverage or creating capabilities within the field of play. Curating content designed to leverage data is an example of how some companies manage and leverage their field of play.

9. Key Partnerships

The notion of long-term partnerships is being supplanted by the idea that every company that uses your Application Program Interface (API) is a micro-partner. In order for your company to leverage its capabilities and share data, you need a large network of partners who have similar goals and values. Google and Apple are likely to be everyone's key partners in the near term. That's because Digital Context requires companies to share data within their field of play. The exchange of data between companies to support jobs that consumers want to get done is a primary purpose for key partnerships. Partners can also help to defray costs.

10. Cost Structure

Oh cost structures! If only we did not have to worry about costs; but we do. The transition to a new business model based on digital strategy often turns assets (physical, financial, human, or intellectual) into liabilities. Companies are rightfully concerned about legacy cost structures and requirements for new capabilities. A ray of hope for some retailers: As Digital Context evolves it is very likely that stores, branches, clinics, and other place-based environments will actually become more valued by digital consumers.

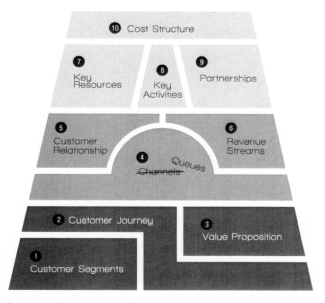

It's obvious, business model paradigms must continue to adjust to the realities of Digital Context. It is my hope that the succeeding chapters will prove just as beneficial to you as they have been to the companies that participated in the discovery processes research that we conducted to understand the shift. Let's look at how business models are likely to change.

The Loss Leader/ Razor & Blades Model Changes

One of the most enduring business models, the loss leader or razor & blades business model is going to change. The loss leader model uses free or deeply discounted product installation to then sell subsequent purchases. If you have been following the men's razor blade category you know that new entrants like the Dollar Club and Harry's are working to disrupt Gillette through subscriptions. In Digital Context, consumer goods become both the point of use and the point of sale and replenishment for a company. Packaging becomes a tool with data associated with the tool. Instead of buying a razor for a discounted rate and then paying for more expensive refills, consumers may find themselves subscribing to a shaving solution, where stock is replenished automatically and upgrades to blades and handles are covered through the subscription. Consumer goods manufacturers are likely to find that the data they are able to collect about usage of one product benefits the placement of other products.

The value proposition for a good begins to look much more like the value proposition for an experience, in which consumers hire the product for the way that it helps them shave and enhances the overall network of other devices associated with the job to get done. Customer relationship strategy begins to be more about keeping a consumer integrated into the manufactured goods' network in ways that support and enhance the data that is exchanged.

> Dark spots are activities or patterns in daily life where there is little or no tracking and thus no attainable understanding of that activity.

Goods manufacturers will use data associated with the frequency of use to eliminate 'dark spots' in the home experience. Dark spots are activities or patterns in daily life where there is little or no tracking and/or collection of data, such as frequency of use, time of day (or night) and so on, and thus no attainable understanding of overall usage patterns or consumer reliance on products used within them. Direct access means digital refills and cross-sells. HP Instant Ink is an example of this approach that you subscribe to today. When you sign up for HP Instant Ink, your ink usage is tracked in your printer. When it gets low, refills are automatically sent. As packaging becomes smarter, it may very well function to suggest the next product rather than to sell the current product. That data will be used by the company to help promote the well being of the individual or family.

One company that is already doing this is Belkin, which is in essence using tiny smart gadgets to probe or monitor dark spots to shed light on the functionalities within them. Toward accomplishing this goal, for example, Belkin has recently added four new sensor capabilities to its WeMo ecosystem of smart gadgets. They are (1) a wireless motion sensor designed to do the same job as wired sensors, but with greater placement flexibility; (2) an alarm sensor that listens for the certain frequency of burglar, smoke, carbon monoxide and presumably other similar sound alarms, and which then notifies the homeowner; (3) a door and window sensor that will detect the openings and closings of doors, windows, safes, cabinets or anything else the consumer adheres it to; and finally (4) a Key Chain sensor. Belkin explains the use of this last sensor by saying that you can clip it to just about anything and your home network will be able to detect as it comes and goes. While none of these sensor technologies are particularly groundbreaking, they do add further dimension to the conversion of passive living spaces into a smart home environment, as well as provide companies with consumer usage patterns related to or supportive of Key Activities.

Direct access to the customer for resale or replenishment means less reliance on retail partners or platform partners. Good manufacturers are likely to be strengthened in negotiations with channel partners. Retail or platform partners are likely to see goods-provider companies who help them to see into the lives of consumers. When a good becomes smart it becomes a tool. Tools that get the job done can become effective channels. So, customer journey work will focus heavily on ways to help the consumer to get functional, emotional, social, and aspirational jobs done.

The Multi-Sided Platform Model

So that's the loss leader model. Now what about companies like Visa, Google, eBay and Microsoft Windows? How will they be impacted by Digital Context? All are examples of multi-sided platforms. They bring together two or more distinct but interdependent groups of customers. Such platforms are of value to the one group of customers *only* if the other group of customers are also present. Since any product that is connected to the Internet of Things becomes part of a platform (and maybe its own platform), we will likely see smart products becoming venues for dumb adjacent products.

Current content providers rely on search and ad models to facilitate interaction between consumers and solution providers. A home that is highly context-aware will rely less on advertising and more on owning the digital or physical real estate within a home. Like shelves in stores, the closer the company can get to the consumer's activity, the more valuable the space becomes.

Manufacturers will have a significant role to play in platform strategy. Retailers may pay to be the preferred data partner based on their ability to get jobs done. Store activity is likely to be integrated with home activity.

Consider this example, recently reported by Digitaltrends.com, of an "at-the-store" function that is activated on a "from-the-home" platform, in which perhaps the first "Smart Garbage Can" wants to order your groceries for you: "The GeniCan is a device that attaches to your trash can. Scan the barcode on a box of mac 'n' cheese before you toss it, and it will automatically appear on your shopping list. Hold a banana peel in front of the sensor, and the GeniCan will ask what you want to add to the list; once you reply, bananas will also show up on your list. If you're signed up with one of the company's delivery partners, you can also have the products shipped to your house."

What better example could there be of a company doing a recurring job for the consumer than by instantly re-ordering groceries and other essential food and non-food items every time you throw out the empty box or container from the previous shipment?
Source: http://www.digitaltrends.com/home/
genican-is-a-smart-garbage-can-that-orders-groceries/

Seven Lessons for IoT Business Strategists

This book is comprised of seven chapters. Each chapter describes a series of questions we asked in the Digital Consumer Collaborative in 2014 and 2015 and then provides answers. We are focused on how consumer behavior is evolving—and the effects on business strategy.

Lesson 1: A Watch is not a Watch

The first lesson is in the title: A watch is not a watch. An IoT-enabled razor is not a razor. An IoT-enabled hearing aid is not a hearing aid. They can each do the basic functionality that the name implies but they do much more and will be hired by consumers to do more than what the name of the item suggests. The consumer hires the tool to do much more than what you originally intended the product to do. Any dumb tool or environment that becomes smart and helps to support Digital Context will enable the consumer in ways that help them to think and to act. Digital Context is about empowerment. The more tools that connect to each other the more each tool becomes a part of an ecosystem that supports other activities. That ecosystem will change your business model.

Lesson 2: Over Time All Channels Become Queues

In chapter 2, we will explore lesson two: over time all channels become queues. Critical to every business model are the marketing, transactional, and customer service channels that ensure that you can share your offerings with your customers. We have progressed from a world of single channels, to multi-channels, to omni-channels, and now to Digital Context. Along the way the channel has become smart and when channels become smart they queue things. The implications for all business is dramatic.

Lesson 3: Consumers Get that Context Requires Data

Despite the constant hacks and security breaches, most consumers share their data with companies freely *if they understand and agree to the purpose for sharing the data.* The Internet of Things and Digital Context depend upon the free flow of data between things. In chapter three, we will discuss the reasons why consumer share data, who the Context Comfortables are, and why they are important to every company's business strategy.

Lesson 4: Design Your Value Proposition to Target a Consumer Mode
Increasingly, if companies are to be relevant and differentiated to their customers, they will need to understand modes. Modes are ways of thinking and behaving that consumers 'get into' that helps them get things done. By targeting a mode for your value proposition, you are effectively aligning your goods, services, or experiences with the way that consumers go about doing what they want to do. Traditionally companies have focused their value propositions on target demographics. But in a highly connected world, what could be more powerful than to be known for supporting a mode that essentially transcends a one-dimensional demographic?

Lesson 5: Data + Content Creates the Package
Companies that are focused on creating content for distribution should turn their attention to focusing on ways to create the Package. Smart Media companies need to find ways to increase the amount of data that travels with the content they produce. In Digital Context, consumers will want their content to be informed by different data types. Companies are used to very basic data being embedded in or attached to content. However, context-aware content requires that companies find ways to share data about biometrics, queues, relationships, environments, brands, and other data types.

Lesson 6: Don't Focus on Loyalty; Focus on Positive Engagement
Chapter 6 focuses on what companies can do to create engagement strategies that enhance the wellbeing of consumers and generate return on investment. The promise of Digital Context cannot just be to speed things up. Context must improve the wellbeing of people. There is so much research that is currently going on in positive psychology that helps companies think about delivering happiness to consumers. Digital Context should tap into that body of research. On the other hand, companies cannot create

context without a return on their investment. Their return will come from ongoing, positive engagement with consumers. This chapter explores why a loyalty mindset is wrong for Digital Context and why a positive engagement mindset is what companies need to go after.

Lesson 7: Doing Digital Strategy: A Case Study
Chapter 7 takes the lessons from the other chapters and brings them together to show how a company might produce solutions that support Digital Context. In this made up case study, I'm going to use a common product, P&G's Swiffer, to show how a company might go about creating a strategy to engage consumers and leverage Digital Context.

CHAPTER TWO

OVER TIME ALL CHANNELS BECOME QUEUES
Digital is Normal, Digital Context is Next, and Tools Disrupt Channels

Lesson 2

The watch is not a watch, it's a queue. Critical to every business model are the marketing, transactional, and customer service channels that ensure that you can share your offerings with your customers. We have progressed from a world of single channels, to multi-channels, to omni-channels, and now to Digital Context. Along the way the channel has become smart and when channels become smart they queue things. The implications for every business are dramatic.

All Companies Need Channels

I can't think of anything that digital has done to business models that has been quite so disruptive and revolutionary as its impact on channels. Up until recently, companies took their channels for granted. Retailers knew their distribution and sales channels. Manufacturers tapped conventional advertising channels and drove consumers to their preferred retailer. Banks were so confident of their branch locations they often didn't open before 9 and regularly closed at 4. But then these tried and true channel strategies that had been in place for over a hundred years got flipped on their heads within a few years.

More than innovation, more than marketing—both of which have radically changed—it's channel strategy that has changed the most in the last fifteen years. And it has affected everyone: advertisers, financial institutions, travel companies, CPGs, food services, retailing, movies. Show me a consumer-facing industry that has not been affected by digital. As consumers we love it! We are so much more empowered today than we were twenty years ago. But as managers and employees in commerce and industry, we shake a little (or a lot!) and wonder what Pandora-like box has been opened. What will be the end result of all this evolution? Can anyone ever count on a durable, long-term business channel again? Are we *all* condemned to chasing the long tail of the next Amazon.com?

All companies depend upon marketing, service, and transactional channels to do business. If you don't have a channel, it really doesn't matter what the rest of your business strategy looks like….you're done! Channel strategy is more crucially fundamental to business productivity than concrete and rebar are to the foundation of your home. So any shift in how a company's channels behave is essential for it to understand and anticipate and, ultimately, control. The problem has been that, except for a few truly digital channel companies, most companies have been playing strategic catch up. There's a new technology platform. It promises to revolutionize a customer's relationship with your product—or at least the purchase process that consumers undertake. And so you try to absorb it. You try to plan for it. And you hope that nothing else happens while you are ramping up for it. But before your latest strategy is launched, it all changes again. Over the last fifteen years, channel strategists have proclaimed two major shifts in business channels: the "multi-channel" model and the "omni-channel" model, which was meant to fix problems with the multi-channel model. Now, if you're the CEO of an enterprise of any size, the last thing you want to hear is that your omni-channel platform doesn't work any more after only three years of implementation.

> Digital Context
> is as distinctly different
> from omni-channel as
> omni-channel is from the
> first iterations of
> multi-channel business
> strategies.

Based on two years of research, dear enterprise executive, I regret to inform you the goal posts have been moved again. In a matter of a few years, Digital Context will replace omni-channel as the next evolution in channel strategy. Digital Context is as distinctly different from omni-channel as omni-channel is from the first iterations of multi-channel business strategies. The good thing to know is that you are not starting over from scratch.

Consumers want channels to be bi-directional. Historically the emphasis has been on companies communicating information *to* consumers and not so much the other way around. Such traditional model channels were essentially "dumb." For example, decades ago you or your company might have relied on ads placed in newspapers and magazines, or on radio and TV, with the goal of getting the attention of potential consumers and attracting sales of your product or service, predominantly by coming in to your brick-and-mortar shop. (Print and broadcast advertising are still viable channels today, at least to an extent).

However, the only way that the consumer might activate the bi-directionality of these channels (or channels of their own choosing), other than actually buying the product, might be by calling your company's customer service arm for more information (or perhaps to complain about a product they already bought which didn't work to their satisfaction). Food supermarkets still offer discount or special offer coupons to be snipped out of print circulars by consumers and brought to the store, though more and more these are being supplanted by online electronic coupon offers. In fact, the telephone sales strategy that was once quite prominent is an easy way to understand the basic bi-directionality of a channel. In a way, the telephone channel is a bit "smarter" than the newspaper advertisement one, insofar as the two-way communication is instantaneous and "active" in a way that traditional print, radio and TV are not.

When companies had only one or perhaps two channels, strategy was simple, and it was not particularly sophisticated. As the Internet developed into a viable marketing and commerce platform, companies began developing "multi-channel" business strategies. Emerging technology gave consumers e-commerce, social media, and the new digital tools faster than most businesses could adjust or adapt. Yet consumer expectations for digital channels moved beyond multi-channel thinking in that they wanted to be able to engage, purchase, and find support regardless of which channel they were in. As a result, companies evolved to a new mindset regarding channel strategy. Instead of thinking about multiple channels through which consumers could *access* brands, businesses needed to create a *seamless* experience across channels. Today we call seamless integration of channels "omni-channel" strategy. This progression in channel strategy happened very quickly. In a surprisingly short period of time the foundational concept of businesses changed from one or two "tried and true" conduits of goods, services and experiences to multiple but separate conduits, and then to connected channels – smarter channels that can in effect "talk" to each other.

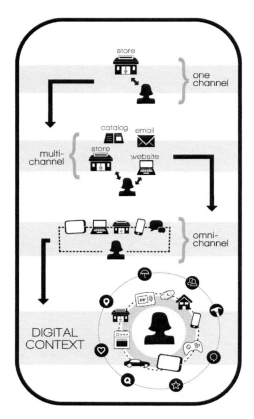

So now we have lots of channels that talk to each other creating more bi-directionality than anyone could have ever predicted. And consumers, being fickle, relentlessly demanding, and seemingly always in a hurry, now expect even more from their channels. Therefore, we want these channels to be 'smart.' It's not enough that information can travel in both directions. Now the channel itself should understand our patterns, screen things we don't like, reduce the amount of time it takes for us to do tasks, and really help us in very tangible ways.

A member of the Collaborative who leads channel research for retailers said it this way:

> *Brands will have an increasingly difficult time differentiating by claiming to have the best price or be the most convenient. The brands*

that thrive will do so by creating experiences that are not only person-
alized, but also contextually relevant. They must go beyond creating
seamless omni-channel experiences and build solutions that recog-
nize, anticipate, and adapt to the unique situation created by a given
consumer's mindset, preferences, and goals at a specific place in time.

The consumer has adjusted to digital far faster and better than most companies have kept up with omni-channel and *has already* adapted his and her expectations. I'm writing this in the summer of 2015. We started researching consumer decision-making in digital through the Digital Consumer Collaborative in 2013. When I say the consumer has already adapted, I mean as of yesterday. Seamless channel switching has made consumers antsy for the next step: the ability to close the gap between thought and action. In other words, thinking and doing become constants, and ever-closer to a continuous set of actions. Getting the job done immediately is the promise of the digital experience and is the new expectation of many consumers. Immediacy is enhanced when digital tools can talk to each other and when data from a range of data types can be accessed in the moment.

The next evolution in channel strategy is Digital Context. Whether through the Internet of Things or proprietary platforms created by Google, Apple, or others, Digital Context refers to a range of innovations that will empower people to act and create a cocoon of data around their lives. Digital Context is an integrated, smart group of channels that close the gap between a consumer's thoughts and actions. Whereas omni-channel strategy focuses on creating a seamless experience for consumers regardless of channel, Digital Context strategy focuses on anticipating needs of consumers by drawing upon clues from different data sources to describe in the moment what the consumer is likely to want or need. Environments, tools and data make up Digital Context. And, as I will describe later, there are different data types, including: location, environmental control, relationship, tool productivity, social, brand, queue, and biometric. All data types, tools and environments work together to support the consumer.

To support immediacy, channels must continually be getting smarter. Marketing channels needs smarts, media channels need smarts, customer service channels must get smarter.

Along with this, sales and delivery channels must continue to learn patterns and serve consumers better or they will stop getting used. When a channel gets smart—and I'll explain why in just a moment—it queues things. You can tell that a channel is getting smarter by the way it queues. Almost all disruptive digital offerings today are queues. Amazon queues things. Netflix is a queue. Facebook, check. iPhones: the apps are queued for you spatially on a small screen. The list goes on. Once you start seeing queues you realize that they are everywhere. Goodreads.com, for example, offers personalized recommendations on books to read next, straight from your mobile device. For its wide range of products, Amazon posts up queues of items that say things like, "Frequently bought together," or "Customers who bought this item also bought."

Source: http://techcrunch.com/2014/12/15/kindle-for-ios-updated-with-goodreads-kindle-unlimited-integrations-and-more/
Source: http://www.goodreads.com

> We have become
> so used to queues that
> we don't realize how
> much they change our
> expectations regarding
> business channels.

We have become so used to queues that we don't realize how much they change our expectations regarding business channels. Channels used to be so durable, let alone physical. They used to take years to establish, require legions of support. Most of the costs associated with most companies' business models are tied to their robust business channels. "Queues" don't sound anything like business channels. The word itself sounds light and fluffy—and unpredictable. But the transition that our research describes—from dumb channels to smart channels to queues—significantly affects media channels, retail environments, e-commerce, social and content channels, and even the home, and it has caused those of us who have been studying this phenomenon to change our thinking about what a channel is. Not only has our almost timeless concept of a channel shifted, but so also has our similarly long-held notion of what constitutes a viable business model. The two go hand in hand.

Rapidly Changing Channels versus the Durable Business Model

When consumers realize that a digital channel is smart, they don't treat it like a channel. They see it as a tool—a means of getting a job done. The first thing a company must understand to survive is that a smart digital channel is first a tool and thereafter a channel. Even content delivery channels— your Netflix and Hulu—are used first for their tool-like abilities and only secondarily by consumers as bi-directional channels.

Almost twenty years ago, Clayton Christensen showed how companies are disrupted. In The Innovator's Dilemma (1997), Christensen defined "disruptive innovation" as an innovation that serves to create a new market and value network (which eventually disrupts an existing one) by improving a product or service in ways the existing market does not expect. What he didn't clarify—but implied—is that the same principle applies whether you are looking at the product itself or the channel through which it is distributed. When consumers start to see smart channels as tools, all of the principles of disruption apply.

Each time a digital solution disrupts a 'dumb' solution, the solution becomes both a channel and a tool. If the job is to compare prices for a new hammer, then Amazon and Google are both the channel and the tool. If the job is to connect with friends and family, then Facebook and Instagram are both the channel and the tool. And the more successful the solution is in functioning as both a channel and a tool the more things that queue up in a digital solution. (I promise, a more definitive explanation of queues is coming).

I'm hoping that by now you're beginning to see how shifts in channel strategy challenge the very paradigm we use to understand channels and business models. The many, many companies who are struggling to capture value in a changing digital landscape often fail because they perpetuate a pre-digital mindset onto a post-digital reality. That mindset costs them time and resources and is often the reason why they don't act in ways that seem obvious and rational to observers just a few years down the road.

About seven years ago, I was asked to speak at a conference that Clayton Christensen was keynoting. My job was to take the concepts he described and apply them to the conference attendee's businesses through a large group workshop. Before the event, I talked to Christensen for a while and he posed a question he wished he knew the answer to: Why was it that UPS took so long to change its business model when it saw exactly what FedEx was doing? That same question is one that most companies disrupted by new digital channels/tools have pondered. Consider Blockbuster versus the rise of Netflix for example. And I think part of the answer lies in an intense (and recalcitrant) desire to define their marketing, delivery, and support channels based on a previously successful business model. Let me give you a painful example.

Not so long ago, many companies who had developed "durable" business models that emphasized proprietary, place-based channels (the local bank, the bookstore, the local clinic) believed that consumers would prefer those channels because of the human-to-human interactions that consumers said they appreciated. They went crazy trying to increase their Net Promoter Scores in hopes that very friendly, attentive employees would stave off digital competition. They called up heroes from the near past, like Starbucks, whose original business strategy was to put a store on every street corner, as exemplars. They polished up new campaigns like "It's time to bank human again," promoting their people as a differentiator from the cold, pixelated world of apps. And they emphasized all of the things that customer service can do for you that digital can never do. But, alas, friendly service is almost never the primary reason why consumers want to get a job done, nor is it primarily *how* the consumer want to get it done. In their attempt to maintain their business models, these companies often misguidedly substitute service and customer relationship for value proposition. In other words they often suggest that the consumer should hire the hammer because they (the company) are friendly rather than because the hammer and nail are the best tools for the job. Digital is the most 'hire-me-to-get-the-job-done' world ever created. You almost never win if you don't focus fearlessly on the job.

Please don't misunderstand me; I'm not arguing against customer service. I love place-based experiences. There is no substitute for a great restaurant with a highly attentive wait staff, a financial investment institution with a smart branch manager who knows how to cut through the red tape, or anticipatory concierge hotel services. And nothing beats a CSR of a company who can almost personally or single-handedly solve a problem for you efficiently and painlessly, say in the course of a single, cordial phone call. In fact, the pendulum is very likely to swing back toward physical experiences over online-only experiences. But what you will find is that those experiences will be digitally enhanced. The environment will function as part of a smart channel and the people who serve those customers will be empowered in ways that only make consumers value them more because they do a better job of getting things done—or because they are now able to do new, innovative things that might not have been possible before. Over time all customer experiences will be enhanced by digital. And while they are becoming enhanced, you need an approach to business modeling that anticipates the world that is fast arriving. Let's dig a little deeper into the first premise I introduced: over time, all channels become queues.

Tools Disrupt Traditional Channels

It is much easier for a new digital tool to offer capabilities that are smart than for a traditional channel to become smart. Media channels are a classic example of this; consider cable TV. Cable, itself once a disruptive innovation, became a fully realized commercial-driven media channel in a very short period of time, but now finds itself responding to new video streaming platforms that make the cable juggernauts look antiquated. Traditional channels are driven by traditional business models and innovations. App, devices, and wearables are primarily driven by models that deliver against multiple jobs to get done.

> Smart phones, tablets, wearables, and computers are tools first and channels second.

Smart phones, tablets, wearables, and computers are tools first and channels second. They are built to get things done for consumers rather than to simply deliver content. A digital tool will always disrupt a traditional media channel, not because it's "cooler" or more technologically advanced, but because it is more "hirable" than a traditional media channel. It is more portable, more responsive, more flexible, and more likely to close the gap between thinking and action. A media channel's only response can be to try to become more like digital tools.

For almost exactly the same reasons, traditional transactional channels are also almost always disrupted by digital tools. A purchase environment requires financial institutions, procurers, an exchange, and buyers. The credit card industry succeeded by minimizing the friction in transactions. And unlike our previous media example, credit cards are portable, simple, and help to close the gap between thinking and purchase; indeed, you can use credit cards to buy things before you even have the money to pay for them. But a plastic card is a dumb transactional channel. If purchase channels do not become smart, they cannot keep up with digital tools and thus will be disrupted—even though they are already very convenient. Tools that can provide in-the-moment knowledge that supports decision-making serve to make purchase channels more valuable. When we were out working with and observing consumers in the field, we often saw consumers who were using the shopping cart feature provided by online transactional channels as a means to queue up purchases for the right moment to hit the "checkout" button, which in some cases, may be the next time the consumer wants to shop. Credit cards, the physical things, cannot currently do that and so are likely to been seen by consumers as being a part of a transactional tool but not the most important component of the tool.

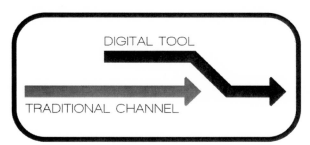

Service and support channels are also disrupted by digital tools, but in a different way; Service is expensive. Most companies do not profit from providing service or support for products previously purchased. In fact, when companies are experiencing financial downturns, the sales support staff are often among the first personnel to go. Try going to into a

Sears store today and ordering a part for a Craftsman rototiller. You will be handed a photocopied piece of paper that lists their "Sears Parts Direct" website and politely told to order it yourself. In most cases it is difficult to build into your business model profitable service delivery post-purchase. Therefore, companies have often embraced digital as a means of delivering service and support because it reduces overhead.

The byproduct of the proactive shift by companies toward digital service and support channels is that most companies know *more* about the service and support requirements of individual consumers than they do about the purchase and usage needs of consumers. While the traditional walk-in or phone call support will likely never completely go away, most consumers have become aware of the fact that digital support channels can sometimes save time and energy—and prefer them over traditional channels.

Still, think about the difference between a smart service channel and a dumb service channel. A dumb service channel often starts with you calling into a phone system that requires you to push buttons to get to the right person who then asks you a battery of questions so as to find the right entry in a CRM system to answer your question. In effect, you are obliged to be the principal driver of the conversation or transaction; you'd better have a pretty good idea of precisely what you need. A smart service channel tries almost immediately to anticipate the problem you are having, suggests types of questions you might be trying to answer, and closes the gap between your question and your answer through powerful search capabilities. A smart service channel will feel like a tool because you can tell that it is working for you. This applies for both human-driven and digital service.

So what? What does it matter that digital tools are better than traditional channels at serving customers what they want? Well, for one thing: this little bit of insight helps channel strategists to set goals for channels. If the focus moves from the delivery of something (a channel mindset) to the accomplishment of goals (a tool mindset) then maybe more companies will be able to more quickly adapt their channels to forthcoming or emerging technologies. If you think that mobility is app-oriented, wait till you see IoT (Internet of Things). Companies that see IoT as primarily a means to deliver something will be nowhere near as successful as companies that learn how to use IoT to support their tools. Let's keep going.

Over Time all Smart Channels become Queues

I made a provocative prediction; I stated that over time all channels become queues and that's not exactly right. Only smart channels become queues and here's why. When a new channel is created between a company and a customer, some new way of interacting between a customer and a company opens up. As soon as it opens up the customer seeks to close the gap between what they are thinking about something and what they are doing (or want to do) about it. This motivation is powerful. In fact, in the next section, I'm going to suggest to you that this motivation defines what it means to be a digital consumer.

Now think about the impact of this motivation on a channel. In order for the channel to support closing that gap, the channel has to become smarter and to do that the channel has to have some kind of algorithm or capability for filtering or sorting information that will make the channel smarter or more efficient in distributing or managing information. Once it heads down that path of becoming smarter, essentially through accommodating the consumer's thought process as much as possible, the channel becomes a queue; it's going to queue activity within the channel and through other channels to attempt to support the consumer's ability to get what he or she wants when it is wanted.

Think about the classic mother of all digital channels: your email inbox. Your inbox is a channel that accommodates receiving, sending, and storing messages. But from that basic set of perfunctory tasks your inbox is going to try to get smarter and smarter; you may want that inbox to be connected in some way to automatically update your calendar, or to send messages from specific sources to dedicated folders, or to automatically send reply messages to people (or to send timely reminders to you to respond personally to those people), and so on.

In this way, once a channel becomes smart it becomes a queue. A queue can take the form of a tabbing process, a grouping of icons, a calendar, a newsfeed, a shopping cart, or a stream. It is a place to hold content, manage tasks, and suggest things. Queuing facilitates thinking about recurring topics and tasks and closes the gap between thought and action, and it is the most effective conventional way to connect the consumer to a smart channel.

In hundreds of hours of observation and interviewing we saw the following 3-step pattern repeated over and over again:

Step 1.
The consumer thinks of something and immediately wants to do something about it. Consumers want to close the gap between thinking and acting. And so, as fast as they think of something they want to start doing it. Any channel worth its salt will want to facilitate the closing of this gap for consumers. And the first reason the channel will think of is to enable potential customers to say "yes" and buy a product or service.

Among the participants in our series of Digital Ethnography studies, perhaps Jake S. put it the most bluntly: "Usually, I'll see an item online or just the thought will pop in my head, "Hey, I need to buy [that, or something like that]." This is a direct quote and needs permission from the user. Then I'll research the item to find the best one. However, if I find something that at the moment I see, I know I really, really like and think "Wow, I want this." Then, I will act in the opposite of my typical methodical thinking and just buy it right away. Igor, on the other hand, envisions a world in which the connection of thought and action is even more seamless and instantaneous – perhaps something equivalent to the "smart home" I alluded to in Chapter 1: Everything will work with everything, regardless of device, developer/provider competition. Everything will be interconnected. Very minimal active input will be required from the user and whenever input is needed, the tool(s) would acquire it via gentle, unobtrusive probing and then share this info with all other apps, devices, tools. Maybe when I unlock my phone in the morning, I will be asked "How are you feeling today?" My answer will then be carried over to other things that could benefit from that information, or rather, that could use that information to queue up (or automatically implement) appropriate options that would benefit me. For example, if I say "I'm cold", all of the sudden Nest turns up the temperature a bit, and the phone asks if I'd like a cup of herbal tea, etc.

Step 2.

Things get complicated. Consumers are not linear and sequential by nature in their activities. They want to feel that they are able to do multiple things at the same time. In fact they often feel empowered by doing multiple things at the same time. They meander between activities, focusing more intensively at some points and casually or not at all other times. The creation of the Digital Context environment massively facilitates meandering and multitasking like no other technology that preceded it, as evidenced by Tamara, who states "I am hardly ever using my digital devices [phone, tablet, gaming consoles, TV, and so on] by themselves," or David, who boldly asserts, "Watching TV without my phone and laptop is a complete waste of time."

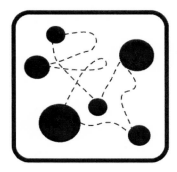

In recent years a lot has been made and debated, in psychology and in neuroscience, for example, about the idea of our ability – or inability – to perform human multitasking, a term that came out of the computer engineering revolution along with related terms for task management like "parallel processing." At the same time, the incredible explosion of communication technology and the almost incomprehensible amount of information content and just sheer data that we are able to so easily access thanks primarily to the internet has some social and behavioral scientists wondering whether this massive bombardment from every facet of our digital environment will drive us all to distraction and into therapy!

But we are by nature quite normally distracted by the things that we see, hear, or otherwise sense in our environment.

How could we survive in a world filled with danger if we couldn't keep track of other things that are going on in our environment *while* we are doing what is right in front of us? Recently there was a lively industry debate going on to try to understand how and why people seemed to be watching TV while simultaneously messaging or performing other tasks on their iPads or smart phones. Some media observers and experts found it shocking that people were doing that. And yet, if you think back to the 1950s, if you were watching TV, you might very well be crocheting or sewing, or doing the bills or perusing the newspaper at the same time. Sometimes you are only watching TV but you can do multiple things at the same time. We are also quite capable of instantly shuttling from one task to another, moving one of them along while the other stays "in place," so to speak.

It is probably too early to tell, but the emergence of the digital context may be just beginning to show us just what the human brain is capable of "working on" in terms of simultaneous tasking and multi-task management. Yet for now, it is hard to argue with the self-reports of our study participants when they report that they certainly think they are multitasking. Among our study participants, the consensus is clear: they share the certainty of the conviction that they are in fact multitasking much on the time. Heather N. states, "I usually multitask in all things in life. I often open different tabs on my browsers to search for coupons or leave open a tab while I look for other similar items in different websites. Sometimes I will use my phone to look up something when I'm occupied with my computer." Laytora D. says much the same thing but also noting that the tools she uses are instrumental in helping her stay organized and productive: "Using digital has helped me complete different tasks throughout the day, however I can overwhelm myself when I'm doing too many tasks at one time. It's great to multitask to get things done and I want to organize myself by using these tools efficiently to maximize time." Finally, Jessika S. reports, "Digital tools are designed so you can multitask. I have multiple devices open at once – computer, phone and tablet. I use my computer or tablet [with] phone next to me in case it is needed for another task. Within each device it's easy to multitask. My computer allows me to have multiple apps open and tab back and forth. My tablet slides between apps with the swipe of a finger or push of a button, as well as my phone."

Whatever turns out to be the case with our capability for multitasking, that really isn't the major concern for companies trying to engage and accumulate new customers. In today's world, however, the fact that consumers are doing two or more things at the same time, say shopping for something online while you are watching TV and texting or emailing with friends, presents a far more difficult problem for advertisers than it does for consumers. And so, we meander. We do multiple things at the same time. It's normal.

> We meander.
> We do multiple things
> at the same time.
> It's normal.

In fact, neuroscientific research over the last 20 years that has looked at habit formation in both animals and human beings provides intriguing support for the notion that being distracted by our surroundings is not only normal, but that certain mechanisms in the brain – in particular, within an area of the brain known as the basal ganglia – are specifically designed to manage, prioritize and control the myriad of distractions that we face virtually all the time. A brief examination of these brain functions provides a startling parallel between the way that the brain prioritizes tasks – eventually habituating some of them – and the way that digital consumers seek to close the gap between thought and action, much in the manner of forming a habit. It may be illuminating to take a brief look at this.

While the primary market focus of the book, *The Power of Habit*, Robert Duhigg's NYT bestseller, is ostensibly to help people understand how habits work in order to help them change bad ones, we can infer that habit formation itself is neither bad or good. In fact, we can have good habits like regular exercise and doing volunteer charity work once a week as easily as bad ones like smoking or overeating.

Duhigg uses an elegantly demonstrate what happens in the brain when we form habits. He tells about lab rats which were rigged with electrodes that enabled researchers to measure and record their brain waves. An individual rat was then placed into the bottom of a T-maze, below a partition, and some chocolate was placed at one end of the "T" at the top. Once in place, the partition was opened, allowing the mouse to search for the chocolate.

You can already guess the results. Initially, the rats wandered back and forth in the center leg of the maze, sniffing and scratching, meandering, "as if each rat was taking a leisurely, unthinking stroll," as Duhigg notes. Undoubtedly they could smell the chocolate, but of course they didn't know where to find it. However, the probes in the rats' brains, Duhigg writes, "told a different story. While each animal wandered through the maze, its brain... worked furiously. Each time a rat sniffed the air or scratched a wall, its brain exploded with activity, as if analyzing each new scent, sight, and sound. The rat was *processing information the entire time it meandered*" (emphasis mine).

Of course, after scores of repeated trials, and not surprisingly, the rats eventually learned the location of the chocolate and darted right to it without sniffing and scratching; ultimately without any hesitation whatsoever. What did surprise the researchers was the finding that as the rats learned how to navigate the maze, their mental activity actually *decreased*. That is, they started thinking *less and less* about the task, and as they ran faster and faster to the reward, their brains worked less and less. They had internalized the task down to rote, automatic, virtually unthinking habit.

Many learned behaviors that require our full attention and concentration when we are first learning them, like driving a car or typing on a keyboard, later become so habitually automatic that we hardly think about them at all when we engage in them. We human beings often reference our habits, both good and bad, by noting (or lamenting) that we do them unconsciously "without thinking." In the human brain, such learned behaviors that become habitual are in effect taken over by the more primitive structure of the brain responsible for controlling automatic behaviors – the basal ganglia – thus conserving energy in the brain, but also freeing the evolutionarily more recent conscious cognitive structures to think about and to work on other, often more complex and sophisticated things.

Well, when I read about habit formation it sounds to me an awful lot like the brain is endeavoring to close the gap between thought and action. It also sounds a lot like the brain is trying to set itself up to be able to do more! And to multi-task. So it seems we may actually have a naturally formed precedent for what is now happening with the creation of Digital Context. It seems remarkable to say the very least, even spookily mind-blowing, how much the electronic mechanisms we are creating and building into the Digital Context of today with the goal of being able to do more so strikingly resemble – or emulate or recapitulate (choose your own verb) – the neurological systems within our brains that have evolved and are designed to do essentially the same thing. At minimum, all of this suggests as I stated earlier, that being distracted and meandering, as well as seeking to multi-task as a means of accomplishing more, are all "normal."

Step 3

In order for a smart tool to engage with us meandering, multitasking people, it queues things. Queues allow for meandering. They allow consumers to sort, search, stop, start, and stay while staying organized. They prompt and they prime and they manage multiple things at once.

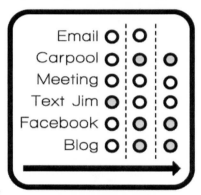

Part of queuing happens in our heads. We spend more of our cognitive resources remembering where we left off on things and less of our resources on memorization of fact. The other part of queuing, of course, happens within the tool. In this way queues don't add to our distractions but instead serve to help us manage them, in some sense keeping them arrayed for us in an orderly fashion. A simple way of understanding how queues are beneficial for organizing our meandering tendencies is to think about the ease of revisiting or using queues that "remember" us and save our information versus the frustration we feel when we have to input the same information over and over again every time we go to a particular site. It is important to note that queues themselves do not meander, but by keeping things organized, queues allow us to meander at will, and perhaps even more broadly than we could without them. Whether or not human beings are indeed capable of some forms of sophisticated multitasking, as queues effectively decrease the time between our thinking about something and doing it, it certainly feels like are doing multiple things, even if we are technically in a physical sense doing one thing at a time.

The most important digital interface innovation in the last decade is the queue. Queuing is everywhere. Almost all apps that have become successful support some form of queuing. No example of queuing is likely to be more visceral than Netflix, which of course calls your list of the upcoming movies you have selected to watch a "queue." While those film titles sit patiently in your queue, you may also browse (or meander) through other possible selections, add them, replace them, or shuffle the order in which your selections will be "queued up" by Netflix for viewing. Not only that, but Netflix is continuing to add features that will help you to manage and refine your profile and preferences, as well as to stop or pause a film and return to the exact point you were watching at a later time–a feature they've had for 2+ years. Similarly, Evernote enables you to capture music, pictures, text, screen shots, spreadsheets, links – virtually anything you can see or hear – and stores it for you to use later. It can be anything from jotting down a great idea you had on the way to work, a photograph of the business card of a potential new client, a travel document or an important passage from a book: The captured information is searchable and taggable, and Evernote syncs the information across multiple devices.

Source: http://www.techhive.com/article/218797/netflix-power-tools.html
Source: http://www.huffingtonpost.com/2014/02/13/how-to-get-the-most-out-of-net-flix_n_4777149.html
Source: http://electronics.howstuffworks.com/cell-phone-apps/5-apps-to-organize-your-life.htm#page=2

And finally, to a large degree, people now organize their thoughts and their actions based on what is in their inboxes, their media streams, their alerts, and their calendars. Queuing turns "jobs to get done" into recurring jobs; "breaking" news consumption is constant, social interaction and messaging is constant, picture taking punctuates many other ongoing activities– think about the number of photos most people take today versus just 10 years ago – and many of those don't even get saved. Report cards used to be something we waited for in the mail; now we are connected in real-time to our children's performance.

Digital queuing changes the nature of channel strategy. Once a queue becomes a part of a consumer's life, he or she doesn't "leave the channel" the way we left channels in the past. Queues make channels become "always on" for the consumer. As my colleague, Martie Woods, puts it, "queuing creates an intimate circle for the consumer. When consumers trust a queue they make decisions that look to be not very well researched and on the fly. But, in fact, the queue has been supporting their decision-making all along. And they feel confident moving straight to action or to buy."

There is another reason why smart channels become queues. A successful smart channel will always have more content and capabilities than consumers can ever use. What the app tools and social media tools have taught us is that once a channel becomes successful and opens its doors to producers, there will be a flood of capabilities created for the channel. We live in a time period of oversupply. From commodities to goods to services, there is an overabundance of providers, options and content. We see a good experience as an abundant experience. And more to the point: a smart digital channel is the most competitive, commoditizing, high production form of delivery ever created. And the best place to manage all of that excess capacity is in a queue. Queues act as a sort of filter to protect against volume yet still allowing for exposure to new things. They don't shelter or exclude us like a filter might but they don't overwhelm because they are smart in their management and release strategies.

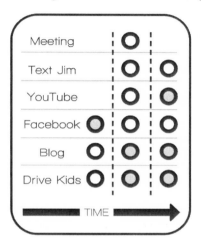

These two factors, the way a consumer meanders yet seeks immediate actions and the proliferation of content and capability mean that queue strategy functions in a different way than traditional channel strategy. These changes include the following:

1. Consumers do not journey through a decision-making process the way they did in the past. If the journey was ever linear, that is certainly not the case now. They still journey, but instead of key moments, we need to think in terms of many things happening "in the moment" or as "micro moments," and abandon the idea that people start and end a phase and then progress to the next. Part of this phenomenon may have to do with the consumer's perception that they may now access virtually all of the decision-making information they need instantaneously from a single source, rather than having to accumulate it over time from multiple ones. As study participant Jake put it, "For shopping to become optimal, you should be able to see a stranger with an

article of clothing you like, a book you want, a device you want etc. and simply be able to take a picture of it. Then, the picture will give you details on the item, as well as a comparison of numerous places to buy it and for that price." Think about car buying and selling sites like Autotrader, which instantly aggregates millions of vehicles from dealers and private sellers, or TRUECar which does essentially the same thing through its nationwide network of over 9,000 dealers, but as a further enhancement gives prospective buyers up-to-the-minute information on what other buyers have paid for the same vehicle. If you need a vacation, the travel site trivago compares room prices for over a half-million hotels worldwide across, they claim, listings on more than 200 booking sites like Expedia, Orbitz and Priceline; all of the information you need, instantly and in one place.

2. Loyalty strategies designed to get the customer to return to the brand should be rethought. If you (that is, the company) are already "in the queue," the consumer does not return to you because you are always a part of their activities. Instead, you need to determine what recurring job or jobs you can do for the consumer that keeps you top of mind. How do you earn and retain your position of "always on." One company that has seen the advantages of exploiting the idea of making itself "always on" for the consumer – in quite the literal sense – is Under Armour, which is designing athletic apparel equipped with sensors and envisions the day when the clothing itself becomes the means to track movement and exercise routines, biorhythms, vital signs, and even progress towards physical fitness goals.
Source: http://www.wsj.com/articles/
under-armour-looks-to-get-you-wired-with-its-apparel-1425061081

3. Data becomes more important to both the company and the consumer. Consumers want the queue to be smart. They willingly give or share data that increases the intelligence of the queue. In return, they want the content in the queue to match their needs

and desires. For the company, data is the only means by which it can assert control over the way it engages with the consumer. In a highly competitive environment, you need the right data-gathering strategy to differentiate your company – a strategy that recognizes that the unit of analysis is not the person but the queue (it's also not the demographic but the consumer mode, as we will see in chapter 4). Behavior across people within queues is much more consistent and predictable than behavior within people across queues ever was or will be. The person is not the telling unit of analysis; the queue is.

Virtually all of the examples I have mentioned in this chapter point to this notion that unit of analysis is the queue: Goodreads and Netflix advantage the queue, and whatever additional information the consumer is willing to provide to make suggestions for enhancing the preferential accuracy of the queue. Study participant Jake S. wants digital resources (e.g., companies) to "queue up" the best version(s) of a product he has seen online so that he can more easily make an immediate purchase decision. Multi-tasking digital consumers rely on multiple queues to keep their information organized and to maximize their productivity. And they also want the queue or queues that are presented to them to align with the activity – or mode – they are presently in. I will have much more to say about modes in a later chapter, but one study participant, Dianna, puts it succinctly: "I think Nike should alter their shopping/buying content based upon what activities I personally participate in. I think they should connect the Nike Store with their Nike Run app so that they can readily promote and offer suggestions of accessories/clothing based upon activities that you log within the Nike Run app."

So, Now a Definition of the Digital Consumer

The first point that must be emphasized and understood is that the digital consumer is normal. I said this before. Let me say it again. We must dispense with the somewhat hysterical notion that the Internet's bombardment of information will drive us to distraction. It is people that are by their very nature prone to distraction and meandering. In contrast, digital does not meander; it facilitates meandering.

Companies and so-called thought leaders continue to debate whether the digital consumer is a market segment, a mindset, or a group of early adopters. They regularly discuss digital consumer behavior as an innovation or as some sort of exception to how consumption really happens. None of this any longer accurately describes the phenomenon of digital consumerism. Today almost all adult consumers are digital consumers, even if only from time-to-time for some of them. (And frankly, so are their children). Digital is a normal, essential aspect of modern consumer behavior, and to treat it as in some way exceptional or an aberration is to imply that the consumer's behavior is not normal, or more perilously, that digital consumerism might eventually go away.

The next point, which is particularly important for companies to understand, is that the digital consumer is any person *who wants to do more*; moreover, a person who in fact feels empowered to do more thanks to the queues that digital channels provide. Queues serve to organize our natural meandering activities. When a consumer chooses digital over another channel, whether it be a media channel, a retail environment, or a call center, it is almost always because he or she wants to close the gap between thought and action. Once that gap is closed, the consumer desires to do more things at once.

During every consumer's typical day of activity, there are physical things that are going on in their lives on a consistent basis, but there are also all sorts of things that are being queued up for them. At any given time there may be a message alert or some other kind of reminder that prompts them to pay attention to something, perhaps even to respond to it immediately. Most digital consumers – and I think this is a very important point, so I'll say it again – feel better about themselves for being able to do multiple things at a time than for their ability to focus, even intensely, on one thing. So if our typical digital consumer is adding items to a grocery list while also looking at Pinterest and checking recent emails, that is often-times more satisfying than if one is focused exclusively on compiling one's mundanely rote grocery list.

We, the members of the Collaborative, describe this phenomenon by saying that digital consumers are almost always trying to fill the total volume of their broader capability for paying attention to several things at once—or total volume of attention. Educators and psychologists have long defined "attention span" as the amount of concentrated time one can spend on a specific task without becoming distracted, further arguing that the ability to focus attention on a task is crucial to goal achievement. Yet doing multiple things at once feels like one is accomplishing much more; it feels like a much fuller use of one's overall attention span and cognitive energy.

To facilitate the interaction between digital tools and thought and to fill the total volume of attention, people and their devices queue. A queue may be nothing more than a lineup of things or people waiting for their turn or it may be extremely sophisticated. The more things people can do or feel like they are doing at the same time, the more we find that they start and stop new things or tasks, and the more seamlessly they move from task to task, or from activity to activity, or from thought to thought. As they do this, they use the inherent organizational power of queues to help them navigate and make decisions.

Because part of the queue is in their minds, they often must remem-ber to go back to some things. But because the other part is on the device or in the app, there is that feeling we all probably have experienced of being tethered to the tool. At times we may not like that feeling. We may pur-posefully vacation deep in the mountains or some other remote place to get away from all things digital that cause that uneasy dynamic.

We all sometimes have a love-hate relationship with our devices and that getting away from them time to time might actually be healthy, tech writer Rob Pegoraro offers an intriguing and perhaps not so trivial suggestion. Citing the "airplane" and rudimentary "reduced-distraction" driving modes available on some of the newest smart phones, Pegoraro suggests that the device makers come up with a "Don't Bug Me – I'm on Vacation mode," which would continue to provide relevant mapping and navigation features to facilitate getting to your idyllic vacation destination, but would "show social media updates only from people you're close to, either geographically or emotionally.... [and] messages from your important contacts as they arrive but hiding everything else." Sounds like a great idea!

And that's probably healthy. But today, queuing is crucial to decision making: It is how things get done in the digital space.

Roger Beasley, chief intelligence officer for Erwin Penland and a member of the Collaborative, was talking at one of our meetings and summarized smart channels and queues this way, "A channel becomes a queue when it adds data to anticipate a job to be done and then helps the consumer anticipate what needs to be done." To Roger's point, some queues are very smart. They try to anticipate the digital consumer's preferences, timing constraints, mood and other factors, and subsequently they attempt to prioritize content in order of importance or desire. However, it is important to understand that consumers do not want their tools to anticipate exactly what they want. Rather, in most cases, they want their tools to queue up choices *for them* to make a decision. In other words, they want their tools to facilitate their meandering and even to help broaden it; but they do not want those tools to do their meandering *for them*!

An important consequence of all of this is that the traditional model of consumer decision-making, often referred to simply as AIDA (Awareness > Interest > Decision > Action), does not conform to digital activity because things rarely happen in a linear fashion. At the heart of today's nonlinear decision-making is the queue. Starts and stops, meandering, doing multiple things at the same time – these are the normal behaviors of digital consumers. And that's why over time channels become smart and smart channels/tools become queues.

I've made a number of points in this chapter. Let me see if I can summarize them:

1. The reason why most companies have been struggling to create value from digital has less to do with the technology itself and more to do with the assumptions and paradigms that inform their business models. Many of these assumptions no longer work in the digital market place.

2. A central assumption of almost all companies is that channels, as the name implies, are primarily a means of delivering something to consumers. We can see all around us today that for consumers a channel is principally a tool.

3. When channels become smart they try to close the gap between consumer thought and action. Digital is very, very good at this. Any business value proposition that involves digital better be focused on jobs to get done. Or you will get hammered.

4. Because consumers meander and like to do multiple things at the same time, the most effective convention for interfacing between people and tools is a queue. Logic dictates then, that over time, all smart channels will become queues or they will become extinct.

5. Companies what are planning for the next wave of digital development through the Internet of Things should be carefully examining their business models. The way we segment, develop value propositions, describe customer journeys, build channels, define key resources, activities and partnerships—and of course, the way we think about costs—will depend upon our understanding of how consumers will behave in a world where environments and tools are constantly focused on closing the gap between thought and action.

Every person within a customer-centric business needs to understand how these changes will affect them. The work we are describing does not fit neatly into any one part of an organization. As an executive you can't simply hand digital strategy off to the folks managing your social media marketing strategy and say, "Go figure this out." But you might want to make sure you are listening carefully to what they are saying, because it might just be the breakthrough that will change the way your company operates.

CHAPTER THREE

THE RISE OF THE CONTEXT COMFORTABLE CONSUMER
Context Comfortables, Creepiness, and a Life Worth Logging

Lesson 3

Despite the constant hacks and security breaches, most consumers share their data with companies more freely *if they understand and agree to the purpose for sharing the data.* The Internet of Things and Digital Context depend upon the free flow of data between things. More to the point, decision makers, social media users, and younger demographics are comfortable sharing data in order to close the gap between thought and action.

The 39 Percent

Even if you are just a casual social observer, if you have been paying attention at all to what is going on today, you would have to surmise that people are becoming more and more comfortable with the reality of data sharing, and more particularly with sharing personal information with other individuals and with companies. It was not always so. There was a time not so long ago that consumers were deeply concerned, even fearful, about filling out personal information needed to make an online transaction, and when the mainstream media was replete with horror stories of people ruined by seemingly rampant identity theft. (Okay, that part hasn't changed). Some of that fear, and some of those issues still persist, but we appear most definitely to be headed in a direction in which consumers recognize that they both want, and need, to share information, which is a good thing for those anticipating the emergence of Digital Context/IoT.

Even among investors, in the past every instance of a reported serious data breach was met by a swift and (for the affected company) disastrous reaction on Wall Street. In 2008, for example, when Princeton, New Jersey based credit card processing firm Heartland Payment Systems (HPS) announced a massive security breach on February Inauguration Day – the historic day America inaugurated its first Black President – the company's stock price plummeted 450 percent from just under $16 a share to less than $3.50 a share. HPS had already been hit hard by the financial collapse just a year earlier, but thanks in part to the data breach it would take the company almost five years, until late 2012, to eclipse their previous high of $33 a share in 2007 just prior to the crash.

In stark contrast, after revealing on December 19, 2013 one of the largest data breaches in history for a U.S. retailer, involving 40 million credit cards and the personal information of as many as 70 million consumers, Target stock slid a mere 11 percent, and a little over two months after the breach was made public, their stock reportedly experienced its largest single-day percentage gain in five years! Consumers were apparently even less fazed than investors: the share of sales paid on Target's own branded Redcard debit and credit cards rose to 20.9 percent in the fourth quarter from 15.5 percent! Finally, despite the consequences of the data security breach, Target managed to increase its quarterly dividend (by 19 percent in the fourth quarter) for the 185th consecutive quarter.
Source: http://blogs.marketwatch.com/behindthestorefront/2014/02/26/
two-months-after-damaging-data-breach-target-stock-has-its-best-day-in-5-years/

Let me tell you about Igor from Minneapolis. He's very creative, very connected, and a proponent of digital sharing. "I feel," he said, "that we are not even scratching the surface of what we can do with technology. If the Apples, Googles, and Microsofts of the world started collaborating in addition to competing, and letting smaller competitors create, develop, and bring their product to market instead of buying them and killing the idea, I think everyone would benefit."

Igor is a Context Comfortable. In fact, he is not just comfortable. He is a High Comfort digital consumer. Twelve percent of consumers are High Comfort consumers. They are actively engaged in digital experiences that involve significant amounts of data sharing. They know they are sharing and they believe that they will receive big benefits from context-aware solutions that will directly result from that data-sharing. Another 27 percent of consumers are Comfort consumers. Though they don't show quite the same level of interest in sharing as High Comfort consumers, they are still very comfortable sharing data and are likely to embrace contextual tools and environments. Thus, combining High Comfort and Comfort groups, 39 percent of US consumers are Context Comfortables. Another 44 percent of consumers are Reluctants. Although they may share just as much data as Context Comfortables, they are reluctant to do so. Seventeen percent of consumers are No Comfort consumers. They don't want to share data, even though they often do in order to close the gap between thought and action.

The Context Comfortables

For a growing segment of the U.S. population, sharing data has become commonplace; almost second nature, some might argue. These consumers want context. They value the experience digital tools produce when data is shared between devices and with companies.

This roughly defined group of digital consumers exhibits some new and interesting attitudes toward digital that may represent an important shift in mindset regarding context. While all consumers are not yet context comfortable, those who are rely fairly substantially on data that is shared between tools and environments to help them accomplish their goals and get things done. Or here is how Maggie Harding, a senior research manager at Disney ABC Television Group and a member of the Collaborative puts it:

> *Most consumers are most concerned and focused on achieving whatever job they have set out to do and if a company/brand can help them accomplish their task in a better or more efficient way then*

that outweighs any concern of sharing personal information. Even consumers who are typically more reluctant to share information are beginning to accept that some data is worth sharing if it helps them reduce the time between thought and action.

Context Comfortables do not automatically and freely share data. Like their more reluctant counterparts, Context Confortables must first see, understand, and believe in the purpose behind data sharing, and they must feel secure in providing it that their information will not be abused, shared without their knowledge, or stolen. Once they cross these three thresholds, Context Comfortables share the following attributes:

- An openness to life logging and the quantified self when the data agrees with and supports their purposes
- A willingness to connect apps so that data can be shared across tools
- An expectation that brands will use the data to make better tools and provide content that will further empower consumers
- A willingness to show loyalty or trust through data sharing
- A comfortableness with the ability to control an environment, or to have an environment interact meaningfully with them
- A recognition (and acceptance) that sharing what is in their queues helps companies to tailor their messages and/or offerings to them

While the preceding list is illuminating, what more can we say about Context Comfortables? Do they skew a bit to a younger demographic? Yes, yet from our research we know that they comprise all ages and backgrounds (and importantly the numbers are growing across all demographics). They have gotten used to and really understand mobility. They are using their tools all the time on their smart phones. Going forward, they are looking for the next level of assistance that can come from tools, and in order for that to happen they need to be able to talk to other tools. Their tools need to be able to talk to other tools in other environments. They expect and are hoping for that to happen and see the advantages associated with such expanding capabilities.

During the summer of 2015 Stone Mantel and MarketVision conducted a survey of 1,209 people for the Digital Consumer Collaborative. All participants had smart phones and thus were, whether they knew it or not, sharing data. Our intent was to better understand Context Comfortables and their counterparts. First, let me explain a little regarding our methodology and then let's talk about the attitudes of each of our cohorts. Through our digital ethnographic research, Stone Mantel identified eight types of data that consumers will give companies permission to access. I will discuss these data types in more detail in Chapter 5 but let me just describe them briefly here. They are:

- Tool Productivity: Data generated about usage activity that helps improve the productivity of the tool

- Brand: Data that tracks the depth and breadth of engagement/ history with a brand and support speed to decision are forms of brand data

- Environment Control: Data that flows through sensors and empowers the consumer to control the environment is environment control data

- Relationships: Data regarding patterns of activity between family and friends

- Location: Data regarding the individual's current location and things around him or her

- Biometric: data that tracks movements, pulse, mood, sugar levels, or other bio data to support health, wellbeing, and comfort

- Queues: Data that tracks activity in key queues such as mail, app usage, payments, calendars, and entertainment can be used to support anticipation of jobs to get done

- Social: Data that is shared by and about people who belong to social networks that a consumer belongs to

> In practice, consumers are far more willing to share data than they say they are.

In our survey we asked consumers to rate their willingness to share each data type, then asked them to react to two different scenarios in which Digital Context helped a consumer accomplish a short term shopping or travel-related goal. An aggregate score was calculated for each consumer by adding their combined willingness-to-share ratings with how they responded to the two scenarios. From these two metrics we could establish a general index for a consumer's level of comfort with sharing data to get a contextual experience.

Digital Context is dependent on people's attitudes about, and willingness to give companies permission to access their data. It's important to note that this study is focused on consumer attitudes—not behavior. In practice, consumers are far more willing to share data than they say they are. Remember that even our No Comfort consumers share data. They are more or less obliged to in order to get the experiences they want. So, let's take a look now at each of our four cohort profiles: High Comfort, Comfort, Reluctant, and No Comfort consumers.

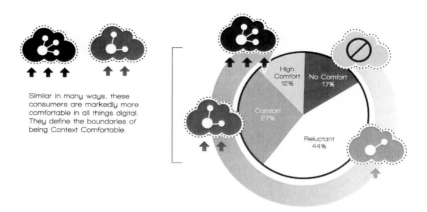

Similar in many ways, these consumers are markedly more comfortable in all things digital. They define the boundaries of being Context Comfortable.

High Comfort 12%

No Comfort 17%

Comfort 27%

Reluctant 44%

High Comfort Consumers

Twelve percent of consumers we studied are High Comfort consumers. They are willing to share data across all eight data types with a variety of companies *if there is a beneficial purpose behind the sharing.* No consumer purposefully shares data if that data solely benefits the company. High Comfort consumers, like Igor, believe that the benefits of sharing data are very much worth the price of giving up access to their data. These consumers show the highest levels of comfort with digital tools and the impact that all things digital has on their lives. They see value in connecting with a brand through digital and expect value in return. They expect Digital Context to facilitate and streamline information flow, providing them as users with the content they want as a result of their brand connection.

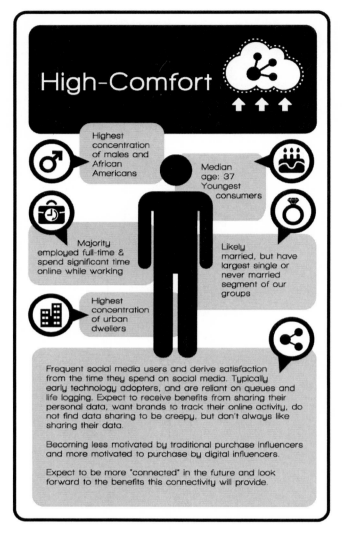

High Comfort consumers are younger than our other cohorts, tend to be more men, tend to be decision-makers, and tend to live in cities. They are frequent social media users and derive quite a bit of satisfaction from the time they spend on social media. Like Igor, these consumers value Digital Context because they believe that they will receive benefits from sharing their personal data. They want brands to track their online activity and in large measure do not find data sharing to be creepy. However, again like Igor, they don't always like sharing their data.

We asked Igor to give feedback on ten brands that might want him to share data with them. He said, "I'll be honest, I looked at the 10 companies and thought hard about what kind of data I'd want these companies to collect. Outside of being okay with [Company B] collecting and monitoring my TV watching habits . . . , I don't think I'd want to share anything with any of these entities. They are all in business to sell products and/or services. I only want to engage with these companies and these companies to engage with me when I need their product or service. Otherwise, I don't want them to have or monitor any of my data."

Note the specific reason why he didn't want to share: because he couldn't see any ongoing benefit to sharing. In chapter 4 I will discuss doing recurring jobs and helping consumers get into modes. None of the companies, as far as Igor was concerned, provided services that were ongoing or created context. So we have 12 percent of consumers who would be highly motivated to share data, who value context, and who expect to be more 'connected' in the future. But, at least for Igor, only one out of these ten companies had anything to offer this highly motivated group. Perhaps companies should just ignore them, right? Let me explain why that would be a mistake.

First, High Comforts are decision makers. They are heavily involved in deciding which financial service provider to choose, which types of insurance to purchase, where to stay on vacation, and what wireless service to use. Second, they are shoppers. High Comforts show the highest level of shopping in all retail categories, except groceries. Third, they are influential. High Comforts have more social media accounts than any of the other cohorts in our survey—and they use them. If you use Snapchat, Tumblr, and Vine on a regular basis, you are likely a High Comfort consumer. They also tend to be early adopters of technology—although 1 in 5 High Comfort consumers do not see themselves as an early adopter.

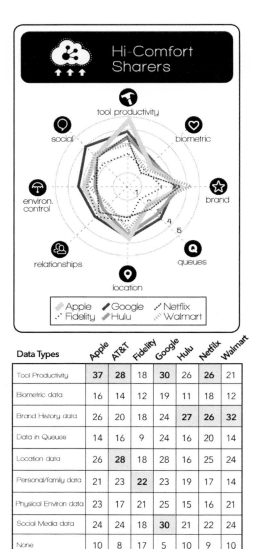

Data Types	Apple	AT&T	Fidelity	Google	Hulu	Netflix	Walmart
Tool Productivity	37	28	18	30	26	26	21
Biometric data	16	14	12	19	11	18	12
Brand History data	26	20	18	24	27	26	32
Data in Queues	14	16	9	24	16	20	14
Location data	26	28	18	28	16	25	24
Personal/family data	21	23	22	23	19	17	14
Physical Environ data	23	17	21	25	15	16	21
Social Media data	24	24	18	30	21	22	24
None	10	8	17	5	10	9	10

Numbers are percent of users who are open to sharing data

Last, and most obvious: High Comforts will share data. The more data they share, the better your tools become. Ultimately, they provide the smarts that will benefit everyone else. Part of the way we know they share data is because we asked them about their use of queue and participation in life logging. Eighty-eight percent of High Comforts are interested in tools that log their activity. They rely heavily on queues, not just to help them accomplish functional jobs but also to accomplish emotional, social, and aspirational jobs. In other words, many of their most meaningful experiences are supported by and enhanced through data sharing.

Comfort Consumers

Comfort Consumers are also Context Comfortables. And there are more of them. Twenty seven percent of consumers we surveyed fit into this group. They share many of the attributes of High Comfort consumers.

When I think about the mindset of the Comfort consumer, I think of April from Los Angeles. We asked April to create a collage that described her relationship with data. She mentioned biometrics, tool productivity, environmental control, social, brand data, and relationship data. And here's why each of these data types were important to her. She said,

> *"Currently, I feel overwhelmed as a working mother, and the phrase, "work-life balance" is not realistic in my world, currently. I am wearing so many hats, feeling guilty about leaving my children when I have to go to work, and feel as if the weight of the world is on my shoulders. And, despite working so hard and smart, I still am just one of the "99 percent" of the world's population that is struggling to get by and provide for my family."*

For April sharing data means empowerment and better control. When she thinks about Digital Context, she says, "I want to have my time freed up to be more nurturing towards my children and spend more time with my family and my extended family." That's what is driving her. Does she like the fact that purchases she made on Amazon show up in her Facebook feed? Not really. Her response to that was "eww." But she would willingly share more data about her life if it helped her accomplish her personal goals.

Data Types	Apple	AT&T	Fidelity	Google	Hulu	Netflix	Walmart
Tool Productivity	**46**	**36**	17	**37**	28	30	19
Biometric data	15	9	10	12	4	6	7
Brand History data	35	27	**20**	35	25	**31**	**40**
Data in Queues	16	12	10	18	14	23	9
Location data	30	34	19	**37**	22	26	34
Personal/family data	17	16	16	15	13	16	11
Physical Environ data	16	16	17	17	11	12	19
Social Media data	21	14	10	24	19	24	17
None	18	20	37	15	24	18	22

Numbers are percent of users who are open to sharing data

Comfort consumers are frequent social media users and derive value from the time spent on social media. You are not as likely to find them on SnapChat, Tumblr or Vine, but you will find them on Facebook, YouTube, Twitter, and Pinterest. They rank fairly high in the technology adoption continuum and are increasing their usage of queues and life logging. They are buying the Fitbits. They are tracking their activity. And, they look forward to changes in their lifestyle and shopping experiences as technology advances. While most strongly influenced to purchase by traditional motivators, they are becoming more open to digital influencers.

Perhaps because, like April, they are trying to balance things in life, they use queues most for functional jobs they want to get done—whereas they employ queues for emotional, social, and aspirational jobs about half the time. Sixty-one percent of Comfort consumers are involved with life logging and biometric data sharing to some degree. About 17 percent have fitness trackers. Unlike High Comfort consumers, Comforts are *not* more reluctant to share data this year than last. When it comes to paying for media, they most resemble High Comforts. They will pay for TV and video but are not as likely to pay for music or printed copy. Both High Comfort and Comfort consumers are less influenced by traditional retail strategies and more influenced by digital retail strategies than the other cohorts. However, Comforts still feel very influenced by special offers and discounts, which High Comforts report they don't buy into as much.

Reluctant Consumers

Reluctant consumers share data but are wary about sharing.

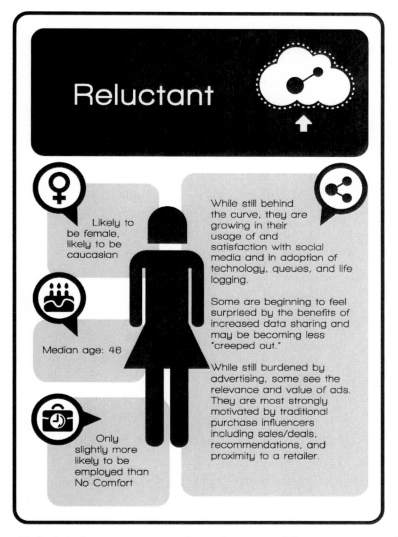

Today's Reluctants are not the Reluctants of four years ago. They are still very willing to share location, brand history, and tool productivity data. Four years ago they might have been unwilling to share location and maybe brand data, but today they see the benefits of these types of data and are just as likely to share the data as their Comfort friends. Where Reluctants differ from Context Comfortables is in their level of willingness – that is to say, their reticence – to share social, environmental, and bio-metric data. They do not think they are ready for that just yet. Forty-four percent of U.S. consumers fit into this category today. Some are beginning to feel surprised, even intrigued, by the benefits of increased data sharing and may be slowly becoming less "creeped out" by it.

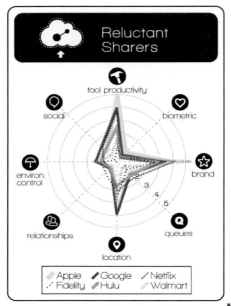

Data Types	Apple	AT&T	Fidelity	Google	Hulu	Netflix	Walmart
Tool Productivity	36	25	9	30	18	27	13
Biometric data	7	3	4	5	3	3	3
Brand History data	27	20	19	29	22	30	40
Data in Queues	10	7	6	10	11	13	4
Location data	25	29	17	30	13	15	22
Personal/family data	4	5	8	5	5	6	5
Physical Environ data	11	8	9	11	7	7	11
Social Media data	8	2	2	12	8	11	4
None	28	32	51	25	41	29	34

Numbers are percent of users who are open to sharing data

Reluctants are more likely to be maintaining or reducing slightly their usage of queues. They still feel that queues help them to accomplish functional jobs but they believe they put less emphasis on queues for social, emotional, and aspirational jobs. Because they are not doing as much with social media or life logging, they are likely not as engaged with tools that do social and aspirational jobs. Reluctants feel they are more strongly influenced by traditional purchase motivators including sales/deals, recommendations, and proximity to a retailer. Stephanie, from Minneapolis, put it this way:

> *"To be honest, my biggest motivation is usually a sale, discount, or good price. Unless it's something I really need or it's an item I need to replace, I rarely buy an item at full price. Even then, I'll shop around for the best price possible. The greatest influence on my purchases is recommendations from friends who have used a product and who have determined it to be useful enough to be worth the investment.*

> *I will buy a product if I am convinced that the cost is equal to how much it will increase my quality and enjoyment of life, but I have to make sure that I am not being sold the idea that my life is lacking quality because I don't currently have said feature. For example, I may be considering a new smartphone. It has a higher quality camera than my current phone, which will help me take clearer photographs. This is something I do with my phone, but I have been unhappy with many of the photographs. A better camera will improve my quality of life. The new phone also has a fingerprint scanner. I am told that because my current phone does not have this scanner, my phone is subpar, lacking, and leaving me open to all sorts of problems. I don't buy into this marketing because not having this feature will not affect my quality of life negatively, nor will getting it make me significantly happier."*

As I stated earlier, today's Reluctants are not yesterday's Reluctants. The study we created in the summer of 2015 is a snapshot in time. Today's Reluctants share location data with companies. They share brand history data. They have no problem sharing tool productivity data. You would not have seen that type of response four years ago. Location, brand, and tool productivity activities are important gateways to other forms of data sharing that can improve Digital Context.

No Comfort Consumers

No Comfort consumers are older consumers, by and large. The average age is 52 and despite the fact that all of our participants had smart phones, these consumers take no comfort in sharing data with companies. They neither frequently use nor derive much satisfaction from social media. No Comforts are typically behind the curve on adopting new ways of doing things, including technology, queues, and life logging.

However, there are about 20 percent of these consumers who consider themselves early adopters. As a group they remind me to some degree of Amy from Philadelphia. When we asked for her thoughts regarding smart homes that understand what mode she is in, she said:

"Again, that would be highly concerning to me. That would mean that some company—and possibly a hacker could control my oven—or know when I am away from home. I have no interest in my appliances knowing what mode I am in. I am fine with turning a knob or dial to turn on an appliance."

Fair enough. But when we probe deeper regarding her data life we found that she wanted her tools to track her usage to improve products, she had no problems with brands knowing her purchase history, and she regularly used a Fitbit to track her health. Always-on location data bothered her. She often used aliases or false names when entering information into sites she didn't trust. And she worried a lot about her identity being stolen.

Like Amy, No Comforts in general experience feelings of creepiness associated with data sharing and they do not see benefits to sharing their data. The majority of No Comforts, 75 percent, do not life log or track biometric data. (Sorry, Amy, you're an outlier there).

A key reason why No Comforts feel the way they do is because of retargeting and online advertising. No Comforts feel that they are much more likely to be at risk of being heavily influenced by advertising. They feel more susceptible to impulse purchases, deals and offers. They are the most concerned about one-click purchases. And over 58 percent want the frequency of online ads regulated. (By contrast: Reluctants; 35%, Comforts; 24%; High Comforts 13%).

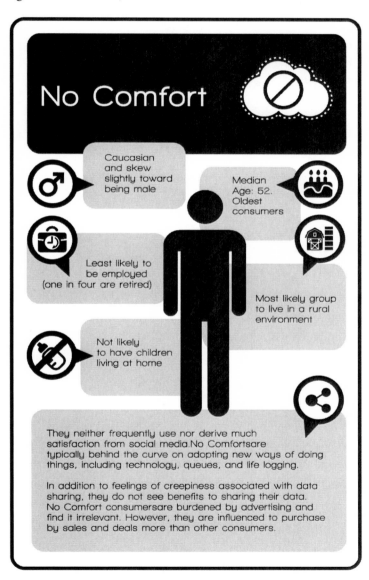

Key Insights Into Brands

As I will describe in more detail in chapters 5 and 6, data sharing is the new form of engagement and the next evolution in loyalty strategy. When we ask consumers how likely they are to share data with a brand we are really asking about permission to engage. Brands that do a wide range of emotional, social, aspirational, and functional jobs for consumers are more likely to have more potential for permission than companies that don't—if they do recurring jobs for consumers. The findings of this study suggest that certain brands might have more permission to access data than they think. There may be a greater range of data types available to the company or there may be more permission within a data type that the brand can access. Remember, access to more data creates opportunities for engagement.

Let's take a look at some very important brands and the permission that consumers are likely to give them to access and use data.

Google Gets Data

It should come as no surprise to anyone that the data kings have the most permission to access and use consumer data based on the eight data types. Google scores high numbers for tool productivity, brand, location, and social media data sharing across High Comfort, Comfort, and Reluctant consumers. Where Google drops out is in biometric data. While High Comfort consumers are more willing to share biometric data with Google than the other cohorts, the numbers for Comfort consumers and Reluctants are low. It's interesting to look at these numbers and think about Google Glass, the wearable product that Google released and then pulled off the market. Google Glass didn't just look annoying to consumers, it also creeped many of them out. Part of the creepy feeling may have come from a lack of permission to access biometric data. Had Google been perceived as more trustworthy in this data type, perhaps Google Glass would have been less problematic for consumers. It's one important factor, at the very least.

When it comes to queue data sharing, Google scores significantly higher than Apple with High Comfort consumers—and on par with Apple for Comfort and Reluctant consumers. Queue data is so very important. In all other data types, Google is a little bit, but not much, ahead of the pack. Think about that statement. Google, the architects of the modern data-driven digital experience mindset—the company that revolutionized the world through search, email, documents, and maps—is only a little bit ahead in permission to access data from the rest of the pack. If I'm the guys at Fidelity, I'm asking myself, how did we score higher – with 27 percent of consumers on permission to access relationship data – than Google? (See Comfort data).

Apple is about Productivity

When it comes to making consumers productive, Apple has more permission than any of the companies we studied. And you can see the trust that consumers have in the company when you compare its numbers to the other companies we studied. Apple is clearly doing a lot of things right. But here's something to pay attention to. Despite the very different approach to data sharing that Apple has taken, except for productivity data, its numbers more or less track with Google's. Whereas Google's business model depends upon sharing data about consumers with advertisers, Apple's does not. Apple CEO, Tim Cook, has been outspoken about data privacy. Yet, when it comes to consumer levels of comfort with sharing data, we see no significant advantage for Apple.

It will be interesting to see what impact iOS 9 will have on consumer's willingness to give Apple more access to more data. iOS 9 appears potentially much smarter at anticipating what the consumer is likely to do next—a powerful feature for an OS to have. It's possible that Apple's conservative approach to data sharing across data types may be limiting the productivity of some of its solutions.

Netflix Rules Queues

Netflix is all about queues. You can create wishlists, see curated lists, see what others are watching, and view by genre. Because there are so many titles that Netflix has to offer, the ability to smartly queue movies is paramount. And not surprisingly, Netflix has more permission to share and use data from its queues than any other brand—even more than Google.

What is more fascinating, however, is how willing consumers are to give up location, social, and tool productivity data to a brand whose primary purpose is to show movies. Why would it be important to consumers for Netflix to know their location? So that the content can be customized based on location. Why would it be important for consumers to share social and tool productivity data? Because the experience of finding and viewing movies that consumers might be interested in would be better if the tool were more sophisticated. And consumers understand that social and tool productivity data help make movie tools more sophisticated. At least a significant percentage of High Comfort, Comfort, and Reluctant consumers apparently do. (Look at the numbers for Reluctants! They are as high on tool productivity and brand as High Comforts. In this particular instance they see the benefits of sharing).

Walmart has Brand Data Permission

While we are talking about Reluctants: take a look at Walmart's numbers. All of the scores for Reluctants are low—as we would expect—except for Brand data. Even among Reluctants, Walmart has permission to access and use brand data. (The numbers are equally high for Comforts and actually drop for High Comfort consumers). Properly executed, Walmart could leverage this permission to gain access to point of use activity. Let me explain what I mean.

Let's imagine that many products currently available at Walmart included sensors that tracked usage activity. For example, Tide bottles might include a sensor that tracks every time the bottle empties. If Walmart could extend the permission it has to track brand history data into permission to track point of usage data associated with a brand—well, that could be a very profitable model for the company. Access to brand history data can be, for some companies, a gateway to accessing more data about tool/solution/product usage. Walmart's numbers are low for tool productivity. No doubt, that's because consumers do not associated a store with usage. But going forward, they could. Certainly, Amazon, with its focus on Dash, is aware of the potential that a retailer could uncover from combining brand data and tool productivity data.

Fidelity has Potential to Build Family Relationships

For all of those companies out there that don't feel like they are the next Netflix, Apple, or Google, may I say, "take heart!" You have more potential and perhaps permission than you think to access and use data to create contextual solutions consumers care about. Case in point: Fidelity. Few industries are more regulated than providers of mutual funds. Finance and insurance are supposed to be conservative. But when you compare Fidelity's scores regarding relationship data with the pack, Fidelity is at very top. With Comfort consumers, Fidelity *is* the top. Just by a sliver, but still! What a powerful opportunity!

Financial and insurance companies tend to think about the onboarding process with a consumer as being the most intensive positive part of the customer experience. It's the time period when you set impressions with consumers that will last for the lifetime of the product. What we are seeing in the data is whether there is a window of opportunity for some company like Fidelity to access the intimate knowledge of family relationships to produce a solution that benefits its customers. Now imagine that a financial or insurance company found a way to use that data to help the consumer and to improve customer relationships with permission to support the customer's most meaningful relationships. For example, parents send kids to college. It's a big expense and often a major shift family dynamics. Imagine for a moment if a financial company could help a family through that transition by analyzing the data of other families who had gone through a similar experience. A company like Fidelity would become very relevant in peoples lives.

Perhaps just as important to note is that Fidelity isn't that far behind the pack in other important areas. It shows up competitively in biometric and physical environment, two of the newest forms of data that are most likely to impact consumers' future activity. The window is definitely open.

So how do we explain this remarkable shift in attitude, and the overall trend of consumers toward becoming more and more comfortable with sharing their personal and financial information? The answer is: they all want to close the gap between thought and action.

The Struggle between Privacy and Closing the Gap

As we have already seen in Chapter 1, people use digital to close the gap between thought and action. To do so however, they must share information about themselves. Even if, as I have suggested in the foregoing, people are in general becoming more and more comfortable with sharing personal information, there nevertheless continues to be a persistent albeit evolving struggle between privacy and closing the gap that goes on in the minds of consumers; one that is perhaps most profoundly felt right before they subscribe to something or resolve to make a first-time purchase with a new or unfamiliar company.

The struggle stems from the need to get a job done (make a purchase, hire a service, learn something) and being required in that process to share information with the company in order to do so. Consumers may worry about the trustworthiness of the company or an app ("Are these people going to sell or share my information with others?"). In the back of their heads they may think, "What are they going to do with this information?" They may also wonder if the information they are providing is going to be vulnerable to hacking, or how seriously the company takes its responsibility to keep customer information confidential. For some people this struggle is more pronounced, while for a small subset of consumers there appears to be no struggle at all, and it should be emphasized that the differences in comfort levels do not necessarily break across any sort of demographic categories or divisions.

Because consumer attitude toward the sharing of data is an essential component of Digital Context/IoT, it will be critical for companies to try to learn and understand the answers to a number of questions that have a bearing on consumer behavior in the marketplace. Among these questions are the following:

- Why do people share data with tools and the environment in the first place?

- How do consumers, and customers in particular, view the scope and limits of data sharing – and its agreeable boundaries (i.e., when does your data-seeking cross the intrusive thresholds of creepiness and or super-creepiness)?

- What should companies focus on to create a value proposition that supports digital context?

The struggle between privacy and closing the gap between thought and action remains a real and potentially painful one for some consumers. And yet, when we talked to consumers a common refrain was, "Look, I've got nothing to hide. If they want access to my data, there's really nothing I can do about it." This resignation, or acquiescence, or newfound openness – call it what you will – stems from a growing reality of today's world: you must give up information about yourself if you want to close the gap. If you want instant access, or instant gratification, you must share the cookies. Or something. To try to put it succinctly, consumers believe that they must share data to get something in return which usually involves making their lives a little easier. While the conversation in the past has been a kind of raucous, yet almost philosophical debate over the primacy or sanctity of individual and consumer privacy, attention today is turning more and more to focus on the real, hard-knuckle issue of data security. There is really nothing that is quite so empowering as closing that gap, and increasingly, that empowerment seems to win out over personal privacy time and time again. And when you move to a position in which you feel like you are an "open book," your relationship with surveillance changes.

Some years ago there was a lively conversation going on about whether Facebook was publishing too much information about people's personal lives. Yet that didn't change the way people viewed themselves, nor did it really change how much information the vast majority of consumers were willing to share – there wasn't a kind of reactionary retreat to greater personal privacy. People understand that they're being observed, but they want to reap the benefits of what is being observed about them.

Steve Whittington, Executive Director of Consumer and Data Analytics at Disney ABC Television group and Collaborative member shared his thoughts this way:

> *We all worry about overstepping consumer privacy as it relates to data, but we need to rethink the boundaries of the issue. We often consider that the creepiness of asking for data is reflected in the data type itself. For example, a company asking for my movie viewing history is creepier than a company asking if I generally prefer an aisle or a window seat on a plane. However, the research we've done with the Collaborative helps to show that isn't true. Millions of consumers share location data with Google to support Google Maps. Millions of consumers share their eating habits with UnderArmour to track their calories with MyFitnessPal. We even link our bank accounts with Intuit to enable account tracking with Mint. If consumers are willing to share their exact location, all the food they eat, and their bank passwords, what's left?*
>
> *The reality is that there is no such thing as a creepy data ask if it's connected to getting a job done for a consumer. Consumers are sharing more today than ever. It's not necessarily because attitudes about privacy are shifting, but because companies are getting really good at providing value that consumers cannot pass up! If you can establish trust with consumers with transparency and offer a compelling solution for a job, they'll give you the data you ask for.*

What we find is that consumers tend to adopt differing comfort levels for how far they are willing to go in sharing their information in return for the empowerment afforded by closing the gap between thought and action. In other words, very often there has to be a certain, inter-connective logic behind both the company's information requests for specific information and the consumer's intent to share that information.

Consumers that we talked to often insisted that they *know* that companies are somehow benefitting from acquiring their personal data, even if they couldn't put their finger on just how those companies were benefitting from it. And they wanted something in return, very often in the way of a more personalized experience with the company going forward. At a fundamental level, they wanted to avoid giving out the same baseline information over and over again, but people also said that they share data with companies or organizations that they like and admire, or because they believe in what the company is doing or stands for. On the other hand, as soon as they feel that the information being sought serves no clear, legitimate purpose, that is the point at which they begin to see the requests as an intrusion into privacy and they become far less comfortable with disclosing or sharing it.

Contrary to what many companies have assumed, it is not so much that consumers are generally against the idea of giving up their information as they are with understanding why the company needs certain information and what the company plans to do with that information. They will give up a remarkable amount of what they believe is needs-appropriate data if they are reasonably assured that the information is secure and will not be stolen or hacked.

The shift in attitude toward surveillance does *not* confer any sort of blanket permission for companies to collect just any sort of data about consumers that they want. Consumers expect that there will be sound reasons – and tangible benefits – behind their sharing of data. And they cite four primary reasons why they share data. Specifically, they want to:

- Receive the right message
- Get a deal
- Speed things up
- Empower people (or be empowered themselves)

On a very basic level, we don't want to have to re-enter our shipping and billing information every time we want to make a purchase from a particular company. And of course, we choose security passwords for certain sites, and then immediately check the box for "Remember my password" so that we don't have to retype that!

Life Logging And the Quantified Self: Evidence for Milestones

Lifelogging is the process of tracking personal data generated by our own behavioral activities. While Lifestreaming primarily tracks the activity of content we create and discover, Lifelogging tracks personal activity data like exercising, sleeping, and eating. This may sound a bit confusing but hopefully the distinction between the two makes sense. The Quantified Self movement takes the aspect of simply tracking the raw data to try and draw correlations and ways to improve our lives from it.
Source: http://lifestreamblog.com/lifelogging/

While it may have started as an odd-looking obsession by a few individuals who began a kind of wholesale tracking of their activities, many of today's consumers see the potential benefits from tools that track their behaviors, activities, and attitudes. Only a few short years ago lifelogging and the so-called Quantified Self movement was considered to be the purview of a few, fairly techie-oriented people. Today, however, most smart phone users have at least one life logging or tracking tool on their phones that they actively use.

Life logging is clear evidence that consumers want to see milestones. Obviously of course, when they sign up for an application tool that tracks their performance, they expect they are going to be tracked. What might be less obvious is that Context Comfortables are increasingly becoming comfortable with the idea that their tools track other activities in which they are engaged that are not directly tied to the app they downloaded. Moreover, they expect that tracking information to be shared with them so that they can observe their own progress, and presumably so that they can make inroads toward improving their behavior or attitude – or whatever – in some proactive way. What may be most important to learn from this phenomenon, however, is that it demonstrates another way in which smart tools can directly influence ongoing consumer behavior. Thus, showing consumers milestones becomes an increasingly important part of their ability to journey.

FROM   TO

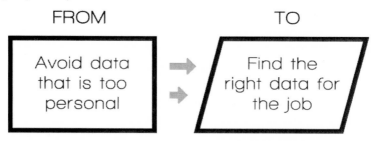

Avoid data that is too personal ➡ Find the right data for the job

For most users of activity trackers, life logging has real, immediate benefits. We love to see where we are at. We believe in diagnostics. We are used to the fact that progress requires data. The day is quickly coming when almost every type of activity is tracked and monitored by consumers for consumers. Consumers see at least four gains or advantages from being tracked by companies: Tracking, Knowledge, Self-awareness, and Convenience. However, each comes with a potential downside, as we will see as we examine each of them in the following.

Tracking. What our analysis has shown is that consumers are seeing tracking not as a negative thing, as they did only a few short years ago, but rather, they now see it as a positive thing that really helps them accomplish more easily the things they are trying to do. However, what they feel like they are giving up, or losing, by being tracked all the time is their ability or opportunity to be spontaneous. This has less to do with privacy, but much more to do with their tools essentially telling them what to do and what time to do it. So, for example, a tool is telling them it's time to go watch something on the internet, yet the consumer may be thinking at that moment that he or she would rather do something else. The irony would seem to be that the tool is supposed to be tracking the preferences of the very consumer who might balk at the tool's prompts or recommendations, so the "dispute," if we may call it that, is with whom, exactly? Whatever the case, it seems that some measure of spontaneity or whimsy is lost if tracking results in the prediction of and engagement standard recommended behaviors.

Knowledge. Consumers believe that through tracking by companies and the shared data that ensues they are gaining a tremendous amount of information about themselves and others in the moment, yet at an equally tremendous hit to personal privacy. A vivid and palpable example of this may be seen in the furious debate which followed the introduction of Google glasses in 2014, and which centered on whether a user should be able (or whether it would even be polite) to pop-up someone's profile right on the glasses screen while the user is standing there talking directly to that person! Not surprising that a lot of people thought the idea just too darn rude! At the time, you might easily have encountered people who stated plainly that they simply would not converse whatsoever with someone who was wearing Google glasses, just based on the notion that it was disrespectful on the part of the wearer to not give their full attention to the normal and expected protocol of the in-person, face-to-face-encounter with a friend or colleague.

Self-awareness. Somewhat related to self-tracking and knowledge, consumers tend to feel they gain a greater level of self-awareness from being tracked by companies and tools, and as well, from the insightful analyses of that shared data which some companies are able to provide. However, as those tools begin to tell us what we need to do, whether it's to cut out "X" amount of calories as part of a fitness regimen or return to and complete a particular task that we've had on hold, consumers in some ways surrender or simply lose some degree of their ability to make decisions on their own, or are "allowed" simply and only to follow the mandates of their tools. In this way, a certain once-perceptible sense of independence or free-thinking is lost or abdicated.

Convenience. By being tracked by companies and being able to see the accumulated, shared data, consumers gain tremendous convenience, along with selection options. However, as is so often the case, it seems the more you gain by convenience and selection, the more complicated life can become because, in essence, the more things you have to pay attention to, or decide among. Conveniences mean myriad options that have to be managed and maintained. You have to log in or restart things, pay attention to multiple things, monitor your own self-tracking features, make decisions among various options, and so on.

What Constitutes Creepiness, and How is it Evolving?

Our working definition of creepiness is the feeling or perception of being observed *for reasons one does not fully understand*. That is to say that we no longer think of simply being observed as being creepy, though there was a time, perhaps briefly, when we did. It is the intent behind the observation that makes it creepy.

Consumers, even Context Comfortables, can be creeped out by advances in data management, or more particularly by information requests that seem unreasonably intrusive. However, many companies approach the whole "creepiness" issue as a barricade that must be slowly dismantled and removed carefully over time before consumers will trust a company to "build a road to their hearts." What any observer over the last ten years should recognize is that definition or standard threshold of creepiness has evolved significantly with the technologies of the day (and our comfort level with them).

It may have felt creepy (or scary) ten years ago to input your credit card number into a website. Today, however, we do it repeatedly to the point of hardly being mindful of our doing it, despite the fact that millions of consumers have had their credit card numbers stolen by aggressive hackers all around the globe. Because the credit card companies have by and large done a pretty good job of responding to large scale attacks, and indemnifying cardholders from responsibility for bogus or fraudulent charges, most consumers get on with their lives, adapt pretty easily to new products and the new risks that come with them, and continue purchasing with the click of a button (or a simple swipe of a card).

Creepiness is a fairly recent phenomenon. A colleague of mine told me recently about how he was going through his collection of old *Gourmet* Magazines from the 1980s and 90s looking for a classic recipe he hadn't used in a while, when one of those blow-in advertising cards fell out of one of the issues, as they were supposed to. This particular ad offered an annual subscription to the *New Yorker Magazine*, and was in the form of a U.S. Post Office-ready prepaid postcard; one simply filled out their name and address information and mailed the postcard, as is, to the address printed on the face of the card. Except that, as one payment option, the subscriber was also expected to write down their credit card number and expiration date right on the card! Apparently this practice wasn't regarded as particularly unsecure in the 1980s, whereas today we would see such a request as downright alarming. In a way, we might regard this turn as an example of an information request that was not considered creepy for a time actually becoming creepy later on as technology (and the ability to hack into it) changed the dynamic of credit card security.

With digital, how we tend to define "creepy" and the newness of a context-rich feature set often go hand-in-hand. At first, consumers were reticent to give access to their locations to Facebook. Now it feels more like the consumer's choice: "Do I want Facebook to post my location?" If "yes" turn it on; if "no" turn it off. Familiarity with the question seems to mean that there is a lot less drama associated with this type of decision today. It's become commonplace. What feels creepy today is not what will feel creepy tomorrow, or in the future. Presently however, what we as consumers tend to regard as creepy appear to share one or more of the following characteristics:

- People viewing your data whom you did not authorize to view it
- Tools that know things about you that you did not share
- Tracking that seems not tied to a purpose

What these three factors appear to have in common, aside from some degree of violation of personal privacy, is first that they operate without the consent or permission of the consumer, and second, they offer no benefit or advantage to the consumer. Conversely, three factors that positively impact, or serve to mitigate creepiness are:

- Advances that help you do a job faster or more efficiently
- Your ability (as a customer) to see the data you shared (perhaps even an analysis of it) and use it to track yourself

- Reminders that work or are useful to you

In October, the members of the 2015 Digital Consumer Collaborative met in Greenville, South Carolina. Maggie Harding was there and shared this great example of how things have changed.

> *This morning when I woke up and checked my g-mail, I had received an email from the Westin with an attached receipt for my stay and the body of the email said "Attached is a copy of your folio as requested" – however, during this trip, I hadn't actually 'requested' my receipt/folio, but on past stays with Westin hotels I have asked for the receipts to be emailed to me when I checked out (something I had planned to do again this morning for my work expense report, but is one of those things that could very much have slipped my mind). I appreciated the fact that the Westin was able to reduce the time between thought and action by delivering my receipt without me requesting. It was one thing off of my mental to-do list when checking out and freed me up to think about other things (like not forgetting my phone charger!).*

What is Super Creepy?

In our research, when we introduced study participants to tools that connected to environments and also supported retail purchase activity, we found them eventually discussing what they generally referred to as "super creepy." For our purposes in the Digital Consumer Collaborative, we define super creepy as the suspicion (or the assessment) that one is being manipulated toward a decision or influenced toward an action that principally (or solely) represents an unknown corporate goal, while conferring no additional benefit to the consumer in return for the data sharing that is involved in the transaction.

Consumers, it would seem, are meant to be unaware of this manipulation – we might presume the consumer is meant to buy the product or service without necessarily, positively needing it. However, the fact that consumers become cognizant of "super-creepiness" would seem to indicate that they do indeed, somewhere along the journey, become aware of the manipulative aspect, even if that occurs after they have been sucked in and actually bought the product or service. And they come very quickly to resent it. (They might even have vowed to themselves that they will not allow the same sort of thing to occur in the future).

While 86 percent of consumers say they are concerned about their personal data being tracked, a nearly identical number (85 percent) say they recognize that data tracking makes it possible for retailers to present them with relevant and targeted content, according to a survey of 2,000 consumers in the U.S. and UK taken by Accenture. Moreover, nearly half (49 percent) of the respondents said that they were open to having trusted brands track their data in return for receiving personalized recommendations, targeted offers, and information on future product availability.

When it comes to mobile marketing, consumers are even more willing to share the places they go in the real-world with brands than with the websites they visit, according to a study conducted by Millward Brown. The research, which surveyed 1,572 consumers who had downloaded a mobile app in the previous year, found that 43 percent of respondents were willing to share their location with companies, compared to just 10 percent who said they would share their browser activity.

Our High Comfort and Comfort consumers see the benefits of sharing data and allow themselves to be observed in hopes of an improved experience. Reluctants are somewhat uncomfortable with data sharing but value customized experience they receive. And even our No Comfort consumers want the benefits of a customized experience. They just don't trust the observers. The Internet of Things and Digital Context depend upon the free flow of data between things. Companies will be given more permission to track activity if they can demonstrate how the tracking helps the consumer. Do that and things become a lot less creepy.

CHAPTER FOUR

WHAT MODE ARE YOU IN?
How to Design Value Propositions for Digital Context

Lesson 4

Increasingly, if companies are to be relevant and differentiated to their customers, they will need to understand modes. Modes are ways of thinking and behaving that consumers 'get into' that help them get things done. By targeting a mode for your value proposition, you are effectively aligning your goods, services, or experiences with the way that consumers go about doing what they want to do. Traditionally companies have focused their value propositions on target demographics. But in a highly connected world, what could be more powerful than to be known for supporting a mode that essentially transcends a one-dimensional demographic?

The Study

What mode are you in? We asked that question of a number of consumers that we observed in January and February of 2015. Using the most portable eye-tracking glasses on the market at the time, the Tobii Pro Glasses 2, we tracked a small set of consumers over two 45-minute time spans as they went about their lives at home. It was the third ethnographic study we had conducted on modes and was informed by a 1000-person quantitative study conducted the year before.

I will never forget watching Angi, a working mother of three, on video. It was five o-clock on a week day night at her home. She was planning the family's next major vacation while she was cooking dinner and helping kids with their homework. She had the television on in the living room and she and her husband were popping in and out of the living room and kitchen carrying on a conversation. She had her laptop on the kitchen table, her phone alternately in her pocket, on the table, or on the kitchen counter, a remote sitting near by, and her kids' had school books open on the table as well. As a part of the study, I had asked her to call out what mode she was in.

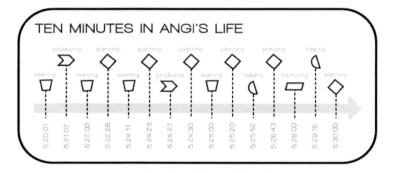

Every three minutes she switched modes: "Now I'm in learning mode. Now I'm in socializing mode. Now I'm in planning mode." She seemed like she was moving fast but she never seemed out of control as she stirred a pot on the stove for dinner tonight, or sat momentarily at the table searching destinations for the family trip. Rinse and repeat, but now with a child asking you what you are doing. It was all part of normal family life in her home and she didn't miss a beat.

Now Dan, by contrast, lived alone and worked from his home. Each morning he would start his day by creating a list of written to-dos that he would check off one by one upon completion of each. We observed him while he worked and his pattern, by his own account, rarely varied. Sitting at a desktop computer in a small apartment, he would carefully read and respond to a proposal he needed to evaluate, then write his notes, then submit his feedback. When finished with a proposal, which often took up to two hours, he would swivel his chair or move to the couch to turn on the TV and watch a daytime episode of something to relax. His favorite show: Judge Judy. Even though he rarely multitasked (and perhaps because of that fact), Dan could easily identify what mode he was in. He had his approach. It fit his lifestyle. And he was mostly satisfied. Dan and Angi represented the extremes of our research into how being in a mode affects decision-making.

The more technologies that sit between you and the customer, the more your offering looks to the consumer like a digital tool or content. That makes sense, right? Now think about the marketing implication of that. You might have thought of your offering as a physical product or a service or an experience. Now, your primary way of connecting with consumers is through your tool or another company's tool, which may sit within another channel/tool. No doubt, you already provide an app within a mobile environment. In the near future you are likely to be a set of tools, data, and content integrated into a consumer home network.

> The more time you spend engaged with your customers through digital the more your customer segmentation, customer journey, and value proposition need to reflect and leverage the strengths of the medium.

The more time you spend engaged with your customers through digital the more your customer segmentation, customer journey, and value proposition need to reflect and leverage the strengths of the medium. You need to think like a digital consumer. You need to target digital behavior. In this chapter I will discuss an approach to targeting or profiling your customers that may raise controversy within your organization. Segmentation is sacrosanct to Marketing. Any shifts in how you define your target audience almost always feels like an existential crisis for the company: "If we don't know who our customer is then why do we exist?" I'm going to poke at that question and hope corporate orthodoxy doesn't dismiss out-of-hand the new, digitally driven approach that I am strongly suggesting.

In the Digital Consumer Collaborative we define the digital consumer as anyone who wants to do more. We see multitasking, queuing, and sharing data as normal activities that consumers do, Dan excepted, possibly. Early in our research a conundrum presented itself. If the consumer is a meandering being, if everything is framed by micro moments that are random, how do you go after that? Have we reached the quantum mechanics of marketing strategy where everything is a string, and strange? Where's the logic in human behavior? How do we organize ourselves to effectively target the customer? We took that set of questions out into the field. Over two years we observed, interviewed, and examined them. And we learned a lot.

While it is true, as we have seen, that our train of thought often meanders, we are not simply responding to different stimuli randomly like billiard balls bouncing around after the break. Consumers work hard to organize their lives. They share data because they want to sort, prioritize, and make connections that close the gap between thought and action. They expect their strategic digital tools to aid them. To accomplish their goals, consumers go into what we call modes.

Briefly defined, a mode is a consumer's unique mindset and way of doing things, or of performing a task (or multiple tasks) that involves a specific purpose and leads to patterns of behavior that drive receptivity and determine what is valued. "Getting into a mode," which is the way that many consumers might describe what they are doing, means preparing oneself mentally, physically and digitally to be productive or to relax, and any number of things in between. In some sense, we might think of getting into a mode as creating a unique environment conducive to the performance of some specific functional task or activity.

For example, imagine that you are sitting down at your computer to work on a research project with the goal of composing a formal paper on whatever subject the project happens to be about. In preparation for doing the research work and writing the paper, you surround yourself with all of the resources that you will need to complete the project efficiently. Thus, you may have a number of physical printed reference books arrayed on work table beside you, but you will almost certainly have web pages open on your computer under tabs to online internet reference sites that you may consult instantaneously as needed. And of course you will bring to bear the body of general learned knowledge you already have of the subject you are researching and writing about. If you are one of those people who likes to listen to music while you work, then you might have a music track queued up that perhaps facilitates your creativeness and productivity but does not become any kind of distraction. In other words, you would most likely want to queue up the kind of music that supports the mode you want to be in. Finally, you might shut the door to your office to try to prevent any outside distractions from co-workers or family members, depending on whether you are at the office or at home. "Efficiency experts" might have described going into a mode as "compartmentalizing."

You will have created a particular and specific environment for accomplishing the task (or tasks) at hand. The proliferation of apps, devices, peripherals, and wearables has made it possible for consumers to create a highly customized environment – and a highly sophisticated one at that – to support the mode they are in. It is important to understand that getting into a mode is not the same thing as "being focused" on a task, nor is it quite as simple as that. Being focused means that you are concentrating your attention virtually on one goal. Getting into a mode means that you are switching into a pattern of behaviors that enables or helps you to do things. You can be in a mode and still be multitasking or seeking to utilize your total volume of attention. Unlike focus, which you can gain or lose, you can turn off a mode, or put it on hold temporarily. Consider this composite picture we created through an analysis based on multiple participants' conceptualizations of "an ideal world":

> *I wake up. My technology knows if I am a morning person or not and supports me with just the right amount of knowledge to get interested in the day.*
>
> *By mid-morning, my environment and tools are working together to help me stay in <Choose a Productive Mode>. I step out of getting things done long enough to be refreshed with entertaining or interesting content. I jump right back in.*

Things that I used have to keep track of—like bills to pay—are queued up for me and I know that at the right time I'll receive a message directing me on the actions I need to take.

By afternoon I've reached peak performance mentally. I can think clearly. I can pause things. I can finish things that I started earlier in the day. I easily switch between modes.

Early evening, I'm in <Choose a Relaxing Mode>. I'm connecting with family and friends. I have no fears about what hasn't been done. I can quickly move from device to device because my content is responsive.

I decide to go for a run. My wearable tells me how many calories I need to burn based on my intake today. My digital device in the kitchen suggests foods for dinner that I like and that keep me in balance.

By evening, I'm in full playing mode. I'm not distracted by work emails. I can game while I'm with family. I shop seamlessly. When the pulse quickens, the temperature in the home drops some. It's all very comfortable.

You may have had the experience of being so deeply immersed in something that you are oblivious to everything else that might be going on around you. And then someone comes along and suddenly interrupts you. You chit-chat and then jump back into what you were doing. One might be tempted to think of being in a mode as just a kind of mindset, but that term doesn't fully cover it, because when we are in a mode we are generally accessing other environmental, physical, or digital resources that are appreciably "outside" the mind. It is the mindset plus the set of tools in use plus the patterns of activity that the consumer engages in that most fully describes the mode.

Generally speaking, modes exhibit all or most of the following characteristics:

- Modes are driven first by jobs to be done, then by lifestyle and attitudes

- Each consumer has his or her own approach to getting into a mode

- Consumers use 'overlays' and 'adjacencies' when they are in modes (An 'overlay' is when consumers add things to the moment that help them stay in the mode they are in. An adjacency is when consumers add additional activities that take attention away from their first activity. It requires switching)

- Because of digital tools, modes can be put on hold and consumers can have multiple modes running concurrently

- Consumers switch modes frequently

- Consumers know what modes a product predisposes them to be in

- Just as the journey for a product is often unique to the product, the modes consumers are in that relate to a product are often unique to the situation or product at hand

- Modes affect micro decision-making

- Time of day, setting, devices, and other people can affect modes

- Consumers understand modes. They can recognize when they are in a certain mode. They can often name their modes

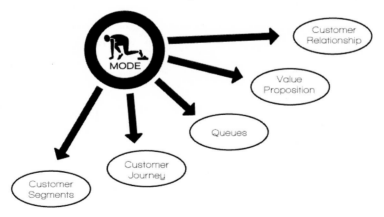

Anatomy of the Mode-Driven Consumer

The picture I have thus far painted of consumer modes – which may make it appear that consumers sequester themselves, cocoon-like, in work cubicles at their job or place of business, or perhaps holed-up in a dedicated and largely isolated home office environment, or even operating within a confined orbit between kitchen counter and the family room – is somewhat misleading, and it certainly doesn't do justice to the breadth of digital's potential. Portable devices both more greatly facilitate the capability for digital consumers to go into modes as well as serving to broaden the scope and power of whatever individual mode a given consumer wants to be in. Today's evolving generation of wearables makes mode enhancement as easy as strapping on a wristband or wearing chip-equipped athletic clothing while running on a treadmill or on a city street.

A representative case in point, Angi manages many tasks at once. It's common for her, each evening after work, to be simultaneously on the computer, the phone and even a remote while helping her children with homework and making dinner, all as part of her routine in running a home. Her family is used to her working on the computer every night, and although the "work" she is doing at any given time might not be job-related, she is nevertheless searching, browsing, exploring, planning digitally in continuous fashion while taking care of her family. Digital is an integral part of her life and the tasks she must accomplish.

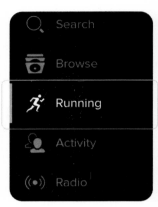

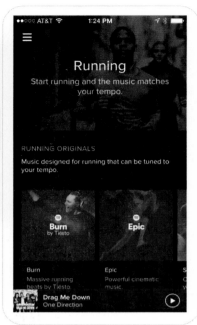

This is a tool designed for a mode.

Moreover, the types of digital devices in use, along with other common variables like time of day (particularly with respect to one's daily routine), one's location (work, home, gym, car, on vacation, etc.), as well as the individual's personal makeup, all serve to influence modes. When we first started studying modes we noticed that there were few situations where the technology actually supported the mode. Over the last two years we have seen more tools adopt modes. Spotify, for example now has Running as a mode that it supports. No doubt more tools will do similar things. But modes are currently not supported the same way that queues are. That's largely because companies haven't focused on them yet. Until very recently most user testing of products focused on one device at a time and on very specific tasks. Mode activity almost always crosses devices.

In addition, modes are inherently personal to the consumer, as is of course their individual choice at any given time of which mode (or multiple modes) they want to be in (or toggling among). But anyone who is running will benefit from Spotify's Running mode feature, which indicates that you can aggregate the experiences of users to create mode segments.

Marketers won't see them unless they take the time to observe consumer patterns across tools. And indeed, when we looked for solid examples of companies creating tools to support modes, we had difficulty finding them. Most that we were able to find provided overlays for moods, like *Songza*, which provides music, ostensibly curated by experts, based on several somewhat whimsical and idiosyncratic categories, like "Having fun at work," or "Keeping calm & mellow," or "Focusing (No lyrics)," the latter providing instrumental music to facilitate getting work done undistracted by words.

Source: http://songza.com

A lot of music apps support what has come to be known as "Browse by Mood," –again a nod to overlays—but there seem to be few apps that support digital consumers in getting jobs done other than those which, as we've seen earlier, help consumers to close the gap between thought and action, and particularly when doing so involves purchasing of the company's products or services.

Digital tools create tremendous flexibility for consumers. While planning mode almost always includes research, and creating mode almost always includes content, the essential "way of doing things" is different for each person depending on what tools they have, the sites they frequent, how they toggle, and both their life intensity and idiosyncratic interests, proclivities or mindset. Digital consumers can change the order of their decision making processes, and with multiple queues to reference, they can do so radically, which is to say politely, their decisions do not always have to be inherently logical.

For example, in one component track of our study that we call Framing Sessions, participants were given a list of pertinent activities and asked to order the steps they would go through to purchase a $20 gift. While most responders reasoned that they would follow what Jarrod describes in the following graphic, others, like Danea and Dandra, decided on a very different sequence of steps. We find that in practice, consumers jump back and forth between steps, presumably based on those aspects of the decision-relevant information most important to them.

Jarrod

Order:	Activities:
	~~Receive item~~
1	Idea
3	Choose
4	Validate
	~~Use~~
5	Share
2	Research
	Other

Danea

Order:	Activities:
	~~Receive item~~
2	Idea
~~4~~	Choose
1	Validate
	~~Use~~
~~4~~ 5	Share
3	Research
	Other

Dandra

Order:	Activities:
5	Receive item
2	Idea
~~1~~3	Choose
~~3~~4	Validate
	~~Use~~
6	Share
1	Research
	Other

This example begs us to think about the impact of modes on the way we discover and design for customer journey. Whereas the traditional model of customer journey describes the consumer in linear, monolithic terms, in which at each stage of the process there is one set of things the consumer is doing, one overall thought pattern, and very specific things the consumer should be feeling and experiencing, the modal model puts less emphasis on big moments and instead helps a company think about targeting decision-making based consumer logic, the goals the consumer is seeking to attain, and the circumstances that surround decision-making and use.

Modes therefore help explain why it is that we so often observe that major decisions are made or are heavily influenced *before* a key moment arises, or might just as easily be changed after that key moment. As we have already seen, digital supports consumer meandering through queuing; modes create a set of habits for navigating multiple queues.

Some of this may speak to the point I made earlier in this book, that in fact consumers *do not want* companies to control what mode they are in or the decision-making process they should follow any more than they want individual queues to make purchase decisions for them. And yet, modes and modal activity provide the first truly digital approach to profiling people and consumer behavior in a way that supports consumers, aligns with what they value, and works across technologies and platforms (as well as across traditional demographics).

Modes First, Then Demographics

Have I convinced you that modes exists as a discrete type of human/digital activity? I hope so. You'll start seeing them everywhere if you look. Now the hard part: helping you to see that technology should change the way you see segmentation.

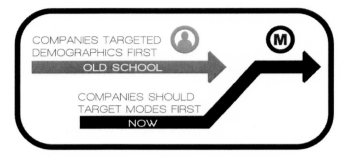

The history of market segmentation did *not* have to follow the trajectory that it did. The fact that we rely so heavily on demographic and psychographic data to create segmentation of consumer markets is an accident of early research activity compounded by the fact that aggregated data on demographics was easier to access than aggregated data on product usage.

In a very famous Harvard Review article, "Marketing Malpractice," Clayton Christensen and his co-authors suggest that part of the reason that companies depend so heavily on demographics state: "In some of the markets in which the tools of modern market research were formulated and tested, such as feminine hygiene or baby care, the job was so closely aligned with the customer demographic that if you understood the customer, you would understand the job." The market research reinforced the primacy of demographics when in fact the reason the solutions were so successful is because they got the job done. Christensen also argues that such coincidences (where demographics and jobs align) are rare, and points out that most major product improvements or significant innovations do not come from understanding the "typical" customer but from understanding the job to be done.

Imagine how *unsuccessful* the following companies would be if they focused their value proposition on a demographic:

- Google Search—optimized for the working mother who doesn't have time for extra steps
- Apple iPhone—a mass affluent smart phone, designed for those with a discriminating eye for design

- Spotify—a hip streaming music service for teens, college students, and music lovers
- Netflix—a subscription movie service for low to moderate income consumers who can't afford cable
- Uber—a private car service for middle class Americans
- Airbnb—the worldwide alternative to hotels designed for people who really don't enjoy staying in hotels

In each case, the who/demographic modifier to the value proposition dramatically limits the potential of the solution, causing the company to miss out on major opportunities. There are likely times when knowing demographics can help with marketing and innovation strategy. I would suggest that in those cases, the insights be used to support the mode rather than the mode being used to support the demographics.

Television, movie, and music content providers often use demographic formulas to determine new content. And to some degree, one can understand why. People like stories that they can relate to. A white middle class man is more likely to watch a show that relates to his life experiences, for example, and demographers have relied heavily, perhaps too heavily, on that as a standard assumption. However, digital content providers like YouTube, Hulu, Netflix, Pandora, and others have shown that consumers would likely prefer a wider range of content that fits the moment and place they are in. Mood matters. Time of day matters. Social networks influence what content the consumer want. Other users within social networks can greatly influence the content consumers want. That's why things go viral. Even mainstream "over-the-air" television news programs now have broadcast segments to report items that are "trending" on social media. In short, consumers are becoming more focused on whether or not the content serves the purpose of the moment than whether or not the storyline fits their age, income, race, or background. Almost every family movie discussion today starts with 'what are we in the mood for.' That's a mode mindset, not a demographic mindset.

Let me suggest three additional reasons why demographics may be burdening or hampering your segmentation, journey, and value proposition design.

1. They often stereotype your customer. One might easily imagine that, in today's world, targeting baby care products to the "traditional" demographic of young, female homemakers would not only fail to reach potentially huge market segments – but would very likely cause a media uproar over the marketer's perceived lack of understanding and gross insensitivity to changing gender roles in our modern society.

2. Demographic data doesn't address micro moments. All current methodologies for establishing a target audience were developed before mobile. Digital promises the ability to observe customers at a level of intimacy neither possible nor fathomable by previous generations. A short history of the way we have heretofore segmented and profiled customers shows a progression from macro shifts to micro activity (see figure on following page).

3. Increasingly, people's lives don't conform to the linearity of an implied and "inevitable" demographic shift. We don't just move from rebellious autonomous teen, to free-thinking college student, to values-based married working middle class, to pondering and retired. Despite all their perceived differences, parents and their Millennials have more in common today than at any other time in modern history. Their values are similar. Their choice of products, especially digital products, are often the same.

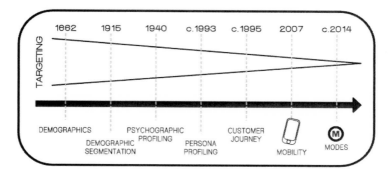

Let's consider two very different people. He is an artist living in the Chelsea district of New York. He's single, in his mid twenties, a recent college grad from a good university. She's a working mom, 50 years old and living in New Mexico. Three kids. Busy, busy, busy every night – with no time to go to an art museum (or any other kind of museum for that matter). But on Saturday mornings when they are each planning their respective next vacations, our artist and our working mom have more in common than they do differences. They are likely to surround themselves with similar tools. They are likely to compare prices in similar ways. They may even do their research and communicate their plans using the exact same tools. Shifting the target focus from a demographic 'who' to a mode 'why' helps a company to broaden its reach and narrow its target. It creates a wider audience while focusing on a more specific situation.

Let's use an example: Let's say Procter & Gamble, a consumer goods company, is designing a value proposition for a product extension for its popular Swiffer floor mops. The marketing team decides to write the value proposition using Vlaskovits & Cooper's CPS technique, a classic 'who' approach that works nicely with demographics. This is the structure of the value proposition:

Customer: _____ (who your customer is).

Problem:_____ (what problem you're solving for the customer).

Solution:_____ (what is your solution for the problem).

And so the marketing team writes something like this:

Customer: Our best customers are women between the ages of 26 and 45.

Problem: Who do not have a lot of time to mop their hardwood floors.

Solution: The Swiffer Wet Jet offers an all-on-one mop starter kit with magic strips and a flexible head.

Now, let's write a new value proposition but this time let's target the mode. Here's what the value proposition might look like:

Mode: Rapid Cleaning. When people are pressed for time and want to clean up.

Job: People hire tools that clean floors with minimal effort that makes them feel powerful and in control.

Solution: The Swiffer Wet Jet offers an all-on-one mop starter kit with magic strips and a flexible head.

By emphasizing the target mode rather than the target demographic, P&G still likely engages those women between the ages of 26 and 45 who really need a mop (remember we don't stereotype) *and* also expands its reach in a very realistic way to anyone who is in rapid cleaning mode, regardless of age or gender.

I asked Ken Kellogg, a member of the Digital Consumer Collaborative, and digital research lead for a major hotel brand, to comment on modes. He sees it this way:

> *As we unlock the relationships between different modes and queues, we can build experiences and ecosystems customers and our partners find truly valuable. In a sense, this is a must. The increasing pace of digital development and lowered barriers of entry force constantly push our products and services to commoditization. Once we understand the complimentary relationships between modes, jobs, and*

queues, brands can anticipate needs and actions of customers and become proactive in helping customers do amazing things.

I think that the big brands will struggle to anticipate needs as long as they build their value props based on demographics. Why didn't companies abandon demographics a long time ago? In part it's because they didn't have any other mechanism for sizing the market opportunity or for engaging the customer. They didn't have the data. Procter & Gamble might argue that it still doesn't have data on modes and therefore cannot size or segment the market. But, with the advent of mobility and with the fast approaching arrival of IoT, there will be data. P&G may very well be better off to invest in sensors for its Swiffer product and observational research of the tool-in-use to establish segmentation than to invest in campaigns targeted at demographics.

Now I'm not saying that demographics have no use whatsoever. When it comes to understanding shifts in consumer attitudes, the impact of age, employment, race, or income on human decision-making, they can be helpful. Throughout this book I share quantitative findings where demographics were taken into consideration. Almost all of the Collaborative members involved with this research asked for the specific findings that we supplied to them to include their target audiences—based on demographics. We happily complied. Demographic profiling is a significant part of the legacy of business models that were built prior to mobile and companies cannot abandon their old models until they have a viable new working model to tap into. I am saying, however, that you should use demographics to support a value proposition design, but not to drive a value proposition design.

Marketing leadership needs to learn how to tell the story of the customer based on the 'whys' and the 'hows' more than the 'whos.' It is only through observing the actual behaviors of digital consumers as well as gaining an understanding of the jobs they are endeavoring to get done that companies will be able to interpret their wants and desires. This aspect of consumer behavior cuts across our previous data-driven and design-oriented conventions for profiling customers and instead focuses on what consumers actually *do*.

A young working woman of today is likely listening to Apple Music while sitting in the coffee shop early in the morning trying to get some work done on her laptop and occasionally checking her mobile for information and messages. She's in a productive mode, perhaps focusing on work. Her setting, queues, and toggle patterns suggest she's getting things done. In that mode she is open to certain things and closed to others. A company that has observed her and the millions of others who are at that time in a similar mode can affect her thinking, support her actions, and even improve her wellbeing. Mode-based segmentation, journey work, and value proposition design put you in her world and make you far more relevant to her. So much so in fact, that she may very well want to share with you exactly what mode she's in at that moment, a huge advantage to you. In our research, we found that consumers are very open to doing just that. This makes sense when you consider the fact that consumers want their digital tools to support the work or task they are trying to accomplish, and by extension, it would seem, they will eventually want those tools to also support the mode they are in.

By telling her tools that she is at work right now, she expects those tools to better support her, to not distract her with things that don't pertain, but instead to track activities that will make her work more productive. I'm not suggesting that she wants you to anticipate everything for her. That will annoy her. She will still want the ability to say she wants to take this little piece here, and combine it with that little piece there, and this other little piece, and bring them all together. But she will be pleasantly surprised by the way that your tools support her if you show you know what she's doing and what she's trying to accomplish.

Understanding how people "get into a mode" has the ability to produce narratives that drive both marketing and innovation. That story will more closely align with sales data, usage data, customer service data, and any other data you have access to. Suddenly all those people who use your product but don't fit your demographics are no longer anomalies. And your market expands dramatically.

Differentiation by companies based on an appeal to and support of certain general modes will likely lead to the following:

1. The ownership of or permission to develop a portfolio of related jobs to get done

2. Broad consumer reach

3. Permission to engage the consumer with content related to the mode

4. Permission to understand micro decision-making during or while in the mode

5. Permission to be "present" in key environments: the home, the car, the workplace, or other environments that pertain to the mode such as the coffee shop

Because modes are not static, linear, or based on demographics or psychographics, they will enable companies to position and innovate products in ways that help consumers to develop skills and strategies for getting the job done. In this way companies will become a part of their customers' lives as they learn to act and "do things" through apps, tools, and devices. The bottom line is that while demographics and psychographics still matter, companies must position themselves by delivering content and solutions that help consumers get into and maintain modes. The companies that will win at Digital Context are the companies that 'get' modes. They will be the companies that differentiate their solutions based on the string of micro moments the consumer is actually experiencing.

There are times when demographics and psychographics matter; but over time you will see that the companies that succeed are the ones that know and own the modes.

Recurring Jobs and Modes

At this point you might be thinking that I am introducing modes as a substitute for jobs to get done. I'm not. Why not, you ask, just focus the value proposition on a job to get done and eliminate the whole mode argument? Jobs and modes are cousins, but they are not twins. A job is something a customer will hire you to do. A mode is a mindset and behavioral pattern that consumers get into in order to be more effective. Modes are better at capturing the moment than jobs are. And so much of what Digital Context will be about pertains to being in the moment and understanding what the consumer wants from that moment. You probably would be in the right ballpark if you targeted the job. But you would be running the base lines if you targeted the mode.

> Value propositions that are designed around modes and jobs that recur are the most effective strategy that you can develop in a digital world.

Value propositions that are designed around modes *and* jobs that recur are the most effective strategy that you can develop in a digital world. Let me explain what I mean by a recurring job. Imagine that you are an insurance company selling life insurance. You put together the very best policy you can for a customer and you sell it to her. Until she dies she (i.e., her estate) will likely have no more interaction with your company. She hired you to do a job. You sold her on the policy. Done.

Just because a customer hires you to do a job does not mean that the customer wants an ongoing relationship with you. Everyday people buy washing machines and toasters to do jobs for them with no thought of a continuous relationship. Until very recently the idea that a thermostat could provide data back to the company that built it for the benefit of the individual who bought it seemed ridiculous. Consumers used to hire thermostat manufacturers the way they hired insurance companies. Now we have Nest, the Google-acquired, Internet-connected thermostat that can be managed remotely and adjust based on home occupancy.

It turns out that many of the jobs we thought consumers would only hire us to do periodically are actually jobs that they would like us to do with great (or regular) frequency when there is digital assistance that can be provided. Need I remind you selfie creators that people used to take family photos once in a lifetime, or only at milestone moments like graduations and weddings? It makes sense for companies to focus their attention on innovations that turn infrequent jobs into recurring jobs. If companies are going to capitalize on IoT opportunities they are going to need to understand when a job to get done can be enhanced by regular, recurring data sharing. They will also need to understand how that recurring job functions within a queue or functions to create a queue that consumers use regularly and come to rely on.

As mentioned in chapter 2, queues create an intimate circle for the consumer. Decisions are often made faster within that circle. While certain queues are temporary or become inactive, most queues endure until the consumer decides to turn something off. Often times, he or she will then switch to another tool that does a very similar thing. When a job, like creating a photo, becomes a recurring job, the nature of the activity changes. The consumer enjoys how the experience can be easily repeated, appreciates that the recurring job can be completed easily each time it comes up, and it becomes a part of the person's daily life.

At Stone Mantel we developed a framework for thinking about jobs and engagement that makes consumers happier – what we call Positive Engagement. I will go into more detail about that framework later in this book but let me introduce the four archetypes for jobs to get one. They are:

- Functional—Help me accomplish a task
- Emotional—Help me feel deeply about a moment
- Social—Help me relate to others
- Aspirational—Help me change something about myself

These categories can help us understand *why* a consumer might want a job to recur. For example, an appliance might prompt a consumer to do something that is timely. That prompt helps the consumer to better accomplish a task. When the job *functionally* recurs the tool will prompt the consumer, thus enabling the consumer to stay in control of that recurring task. Done well, the consumer will value the prompt and keep the tool turned on.

Now let's say that the benefit the consumer seeks from the tool is more emotional in nature. Perhaps the recurring job is tied to a moment that matters to the consumer. As we tracked consumers we noticed, for example, that most social media users checked into their social media tools first thing in the morning as a way of feeling good about themselves. It was a pick me up. When the job to get done is emotionally recurring, the consumer will engage with the tool to change or improve mood. Companies that understand this will work to develop engagement strategies that turn their recurring jobs into mood improvement solutions.

If a consumer hires a company to do a socially recurring job, then the focus will be on the timely sharing of information. Most companies today understand how a social job becomes a recurring job. They see examples everywhere, of which Facebook and Instagram are the most enormously obvious ones.

The last category is aspirational jobs to get done. When you regularly use a tool to elevate your game—think Fitbit—then the job becomes aspirationally recurring. The primary reason that the company is hired becomes to help progress the individual toward a goal.

> When you
> regularly use a tool to
> elevate your game—think
> Fitbit—then the job
> becomes aspirationally
> recurring.

Most tools have more than one way that the job becomes recurring. For each type of recurring job there are different types of data that are shared between the company and the consumer. The ongoing flow of data between a company and its customers is one of the best signs that the customer values the recurring job. Doing recurring jobs keeps consumers in the queue, reinforces an intimate circle with the customer, and dramatically increases the relevancy of the product to the customer.

When you design for recurring jobs and you understand the modes that consumers are most likely to be in when doing recurring jobs, you know a lot about your customer. When we observed consumers over a significant period of time (at least 1+ hours), we discovered that often times consumers are not even aware of certain things they are doing because they come so naturally. For example, unless it is pointed out to them, consumers are often not aware that they are switching modes. As one of our research participants put it, "I'm not sure what you mean by 'switching modes,' but I switch gears several times a minute." One observable pattern, for example, is that after focusing on modes that are productive or performance oriented, and thus presumably effort-intensive, consumers often switch to modes that are more relaxing and less performance-critical. This back and forth between productivity modes and relaxing modes helps the consumer to do more and still enjoy what he or she is doing. It may have the effect of easing the pressure to perform at a high level.

Nor is staying in a given mode the primary goal of consumers. Similar to trends in multitasking, consumers are quite open to adjacencies—different activities that happen concurrent with each other—and rarely prefer to stay in one mode for long periods of time. The decision to add activities clearly depends on the "importance" and perhaps also on the intensity or urgency of the tasks at hand. We find that consumers are generally more aware of consciously staying in modal activities that require more serious or dedicated attention (like driving, reading, or attending more formal events such as a business conference or personal improvement seminar) than ones for which casual attention is sufficient (like talking on the phone, preparing dinner, or watching TV).

One of our study participants, Amy W., a married, full-time working woman with a husband and two children, reflected, interestingly enough, on how distracting digital can be – and how she copes with that – when we asked her how she can get herself into a mode or modes so that she can be both productive and connected. Her response initially indicates a judicious approach to modal activity:

> "Well, many times when I am being productive I am still connected. A lot of what I do to produce is online or on a computer, so I am engaged in technology. However, if I am on Skype for a conference call, then my phone and email are "off." This allows me to focus. If I need to work on a project that requires my full attention, I block out time so I don't have to answer my phone or emails. I schedule time to answer emails, pay bills, etc. Of course, then I am productive and still connected, but the difference is I am focused."

Yet, Amy engages in a partitioning of sorts when it comes to devoting attention to her children. "I guess my point was that I see a mom at a kid's hockey game and she is constantly on her phone – responding to texts and getting notifications and posting to Facebook. I feel bad for her kids. Technology is awesome especially for being productive, but there are times when multi-tasking is harmful."

Finally Amy acknowledges that she likes to be both productive and connected, that "multi-tasking is… possible," while jumping in and out of different modes, stating that, "An example of when I CAN be connected and be productive (or creative) is when I listen to online radio or a podcast while cleaning, or maybe doing a craft or something with the kids. It is absolutely possible to multi-task, and I love having music playing. I also find when I am waiting (like for instance we have to get to my son's hockey games early so he can warm up), those 20 minutes are heaven. I will update my calendar, send out any texts, search for coupons, etc. I love having my phone so I can get all of that done. It is pretty sad when I am excited to lock myself in my car for 20 minutes of peace, but any mom (or dad) who has busy kids will understand what I am talking about."

What is insightful about Amy's last remarks here is that her sense of distraction may have more to do with balancing home life, work responsibilities, and her children's activities than it does with digital per se as a distractive force. However, this explanation also supports the conjecture that channels that more effectively support her when she is in different modes would be of great benefit in helping her to remain more connected and be more productive, by making those aspects more seamless, and accordingly allow her to feel less distracted – and more in control – overall.

While it may seem paradoxical to both the notion that consumers are often unaware of their own mode-switching and their apparent ambivalence about which one they are in at any given time, it is also clear that in order for individuals to be in most modes requires intention and focus, which in turn leads to a certain cadence in the individual's behavior. Consumers will often start to operate in one mode but then add another – or their life circumstances in the moment may require them to be juggling multiple modes at the same time. Thus, consumers want a kind of opt-out button that provides the ability to pause modes temporarily, and then the ability to effortlessly come back to them later.

Companies may thus have more ability to support modes than might have been previously assumed; for example, by advantaging the ability to save a search, or to freeze or preserve a set of activities, the ability exists to gently remind a consumer of an activity or purchase that he or she started but did not finish. Companies may even be able to influence the modes consumers are in by gaining an understanding of the particular kind of content that consumers are receptive to depending on their mode, and how that content might be presented in an intriguing way that encourages a consumer to change modes.

Companies seeking to influence the mode that consumers are in should proceed with caution, however. Nobody likes the hard-sell sales pitch; it is likely that digital consumers who come to think that a company is trying to coerce them into a certain mode will be similarly turned off. One of the important factors we have noticed in our research is that, for some consumers, their receptivity to content increases when the content is smart. Thus, companies that use appropriate data types to serve content for a given mode are more likely to influence the mode (or mode switching) without any backlash. It may also be the case that consumers will be more receptive to content or "suggestible" when they are in certain specific modes but not in others.

Given that our study participant Keira K. is also married with one teenage daughter, and working full-time with the added pressure of being self-employed, it comes as no surprise that she would love for her tools to act almost like a personal/professional secretary. She describes an ideal environment as one that supports her on multiple, time-shifting levels:

> *"I want technology to help me manage my modes, mainly assist me in managing time. But, I want the technology to be more advanced than the traditional time technology I currently have, like my calendar.*
> *I'd like the app to help organize my day and keep me on track for the tasks I have, while taking into account the various modes I need to go through in order to get my work completed. It could track my typical daily modes and set up a schedule for my tasks (based upon the order they should be completed taking into account my modes). If I have an atypical day, the app could track my modes and readjust my schedule for me. The environment is going to have to do a couple of things such as nudge me to collect information regarding what mode I am in.*

Then it is going to have to collect data from me regarding how long it takes me to complete various tasks (for example, how long does it normally take me to set up my calendar for the day). Then, the environment will need to "crunch the number" and come up with times when I most productive to complete various tasks depending on what mode I'm in, and how long it should take me to complete said task."

We might also crucially note in Keira's response her substantial willingness to rely on the tools that would help her manage her time and tasks more effectively, and even to make adjustments as needed, which will of course require her to share an enormous amount of data with her tools. Those tools, she specifically states, must *"collect information regarding what mode I am in"* and even tell her when she is *"most productive to complete various tasks depending on what mode"* she is in! It's a scenario that she sees as highly supportive, yet critically, without being intrusive.

Because companies have not yet developed a mode mindset, they use their tools to target decision-making without actually supporting decision-making. Aside from promotional techniques, most companies have no mechanisms to help the consumer progress toward a positive outcome. As we saw in Chapter 2 with respect to channels and queues, digital consumers want to be presented with numerous options to choose from, but they want to actually make the choice for themselves.

Let's go back to our new model for value propositions. I suggested that value proposition design based on modes includes three elements: the mode, the job, and the solution. Let's now modify that second element to include recurring activity and I think you will see how this type of thinking aligns with Digital Context/IoT.

Mode: Rapid Cleaning. When people are pressed for time and want to clean up.

Job: People hire tools that clean floors with minimal effort that makes them feel powerful and in control.

Recurrence: Each time they clean they like having disposable floor wipes and replenished liquid cleaner.

Solution: The Swiffer Wet Jet offers an all-on-one mop starter kit with magic strips and a flexible head. When the packet of magic strips runs out a button lights up on the packaging that when pressed reorders more strips. The same feature is available for liquid cleaner.

Digital Context will support recurrence. The companies that will be most successful are those that find ways to use IoT to support solutions that recur. One more thought: companies want consumers to share data with them. Our research indicates that when a consumer is in a mode, he or she is sharing a lot of data, and the type of data that is exchanged appears to have more to do with what the consumer needs than being simply a matter of what information that consumer is willing to reveal. Thus, it stands to reason that being in a mode makes the digital consumer more suggestible with respect to things that relate to that mode, including the purchase of goods or services that advance their progress. In this way, modes offer a tremendous opportunity for innovative companies hungry for growth.

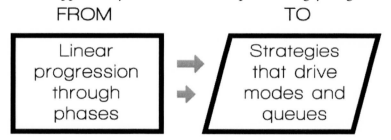

Eleven Important Modes

To date we have studied eleven modes that have general application to consumer-facing businesses. They are:

- Improving
- Browsing & Exploring
- Creating
- Giving and Sharing

- Learning
- Organizing
- Planning
- Playing
- Producing
- Socializing
- Competing

As a part of our research we conducted a 1,000 person survey and asked participants whether or not they were in one of the above modes the day before. You will see the percentage of people who said they were in a particular mode 'yesterday' throughout this section.

There are other modes. Depending on the product, you may need a much more specific set of well-defined modes to describe your customer's activity. And every company needs to understand the modes that matter most to their products. But let's take a little closer look at these:

Improving Mode

When a consumer is in improving mode, he or she is focused on personal progress toward a goal. Digital Context/IoT can support improving mode by tracking consumer **milestones**, by networking more solutions that help consumers improve across categories (health, athletics, shopping, and self improvement), and by sharing data with consumer that describes effectively how he or she can improve. Expectations of consumers for solutions that support improving mode include:

- Health—Take biometric data and use it to 'challenge me' to optimize well-being

- Diets—Fully track and monitor food intake (may include everything from calories to antioxidants to omega-3's and so on). Set goals and make recommendations

- Athletics—Wearables and sensors to track, collect and analyze data to map paths for improvement

- Life Skills—To track and improve personal performance on a wide variety of life skills

There are some wonderful tools being developed today that focus on self-improvement. One is Golf Game, which provides golfers a revolutionary way to track their shot performance. Shot by shot, it records all their stats so they can visualize their game like never before and enjoy it on a whole new level. It gives them the insights they need to start shaving strokes off their golf game. It even lets them share their progress – or that killer drive – with friends, family and followers on social media, or compare how they stack up against other players in their handicap bracket.

Browsing & Exploring Mode
Seventy percent of consumers were in browsing & exploring mode yesterday. Unlike other, more definitively goal-centric modes, browsing & exploring mode is decidedly unstructured, frequently a default state, and integrated into much of what consumers do on a regular basis, including as a means to support other modes. We all understand the power of this mode in Web browsers. A likely impact of Digital Context/IoT on consumer behavior is that environments (stores, homes, restaurants, airports, etc.) will become venues for browsing & exploring. Smart environments should support enhanced browsing. We see evidence that NFL and MLB stadiums are beginning to understand the power of supporting browsing & exploring while in a stadium. More venues need to follow suit. In fact, in September of 2015, the oceanfront town of Seaside Park claimed to have become the first New Jersey shore community to make free Wi-Fi available along its entire 1.6-mile long beach for vacationers and locals alike. In announcing the activation of what he called "Connected Seaside Park," Mayor Robert Matthies said the decision was based on a "scientific" survey conducted by travel industry giant Expedia which found that "the *number*

one reason for both businesses and leisure travelers to choose the locations that they do was free Wi-Fi."
Source: http://nj1015.com/seaside-park-is-1st-nj-beach-to-offer-free-wi-fi-service/

Michael Baskin, a Stone Mantel lead strategist, points out that Nordstrom is making headway in supporting environment-based browsing & exploring. The Nordstrom Connected Store uses an interactive mirror to track all of the items in the room and identify other sizes and colors that are available in the store. For now, associates will have to scan barcodes of the shopper's items with an industrial scanner outside the fitting room to get the correct information on the screen; however, in the future, it may be possible to use RFID tags. The mirror will make recommendations to provide cross-selling opportunities. The experience also has check-out and post-transaction components. For instance, shoppers will be able to request an associate from inside the room to pay for items through the mirror. If all goes well for Nordstrom's vision, associates will be able to stay in touch with shoppers through their own app, which allows them to get clothing requests from the shopper and provides insights on the shopper for future visits.

A physical retailer who doesn't support browsing & exploring will likely fail in the future.

Creating Mode
While only 24 percent of consumers were in creating mode yesterday, there is likely to be continued and growing interest by consumers to spend more time in this productive mode. Consumers will increasingly blur the lines between the physical experience and the virtual when in creating mode. Curating, storytelling, and publishing are activities that consumers often associate with being a part of creating mode.

GoPro and Pinterest are tools that consumers often associate with creating mode. The structuring and sorting of content to be shared with others feels like creating something to consumers. We anticipate that frequent activities within the home that are enhanced by Digital Context/

IoT will feel more like creating modes. These include: food preparation, seasonal home decorating, and music and movie curating for family.

> GoPro and Pinterest are tools that consumers often associate with creating mode.

Socializing Mode

In our first round of research, socializing mode was also lumped in with Giving and Sharing modes. Fifty two percent of consumers were in some form of these modes yesterday. Socializing mode, however, is all about context. It situates the consumer amongst a group of friends, family, and co-workers. Socializing mode requires people who are engaged with each other in conversations. Tools can enhance socializing mode, and we believe that many companies could benefit from understanding and supporting this mode more effectively. Think about how the following tools could enhance socializing:

- Maps: Create a sense of community from location data

- Wearables: Connect biometric and performance data to share with friends and family

- Smart Televisions: Provide the ability to view and share with a limited group of people real time and captured video content

- Laptop: Provide a lifelogging tool that supports one's social life and provides personal analytics about your friendship networks

Over the next three years, consumers will expect greater controls and flexibility in how they engage in socializing mode. For example, while dating sites have been around for a long time, *happn.com* offers a new mobile app that uses your phone's location to show you potential matches simply among the people you cross paths with, no matter where you are in the world. Similarly, the app *Highlight.com* allows users to learn more about the people around them without the principal goal of dating. If someone standing near you also has the app, *Highlight* will display that person's profile – name, photos, mutual friends, and anything they have chosen to share – on your mobile device, enabling you to see what you have in common, and presumably information you might use to make an introduction. In addition, if your friends are nearby, *Highlight* with notify you of their presence.

Giving and Sharing Modes

When we started studying these related dual modes we hypothesized that they were the same mode, and consequently our quantitative research asked questions that lumped these to modes together. Subsequent qualitative work suggests that they are distinct mindsets and behavioral patterns. Consumers spend a significant amount of time in these two modes combined. Yesterday, 52 percent of consumers were in one of these two modes.

Giving mode refers to the mindset and patterns associated with nurturing, taking care of, or supporting things, places, or people. Sharing mode refers to the mindsets and patterns associated with expressing oneself or gifting information to others. Consumers share all of the time. There is a high level of frequency for this mode because companies value this activity over other types of modes. Both giving and sharing are perceived by consumers, ideally, to be forms of pleasant relaxation. Supporting these modes should bring calmness and enjoyment. They can be in these modes while they are in other modes. Perhaps no one participant in our studies exemplified these qualitative emotional aspects more than Liz, who explained, "I'm kind of like my mother, I put a lot of thought into the gifts that I buy, So I enjoy that process – the thinking of ideas, researching ideas. Whereas I know some people get stressed out, but I get enjoyment in thinking of what other people might want and completing the transaction."

Learning Mode

Forty-five percent of consumers were in learning mode yesterday. Learning mode is a highly productive mode to be in, and very palpably so for consumers, who therefore tend to be more intensely focused and engaged when they are in it. Things that can companies can do to enhance learning mode include:

- Support the ability to research a topic and construct information based on location – for example, "Am I learning at home or at work?"
- Support lifelong learning and reminding of things learned
- Support knowing where or who to connect to when learning

Most companies will have some interest in supporting learning mode because consumers are most open to making a purchase when they are in learning mode. While we might point to various "How to" websites offered by the big home improvement companies like Lowe's and Home Depot (which of course highlight the in-store and online purchase products those companies offer to do the job), the fact is that YouTube is loaded with hundreds of thousands of "How to" videos that instruct people on just every imaginable task or topic, all of which can be seen at least in a passive sense as supporting learning mode.

Organizing Mode

The mindset and patterns associated with organizing mode include sorting, cleaning up, scheduling, and prioritizing. Fifty percent of consumers were in organizing mode yesterday. This mode too feels highly productive to consumers. It is also one of the higher paced modes. That is, consumers like to feel as though they are making fast progress in a short amount of time. Most consumers organize while they do other things. It does not require a lot of focus, nor, it seems, do consumers want to spend a lot of time "getting organized."

Organizing mode can trigger repurchasing or replenishment to-do's. We think that solutions like Amazon Dash are likely to be successful if they help consumers feel like they are staying organized. Dash, which as of the writing of this book is in beta tests, is a series of consumer goods brand buttons that can be placed throughout the house. When you push the button the tool connects with Amazon's shopping site and automatically sends you a replenishment of the specific consumer good product, like laundry detergent , health care products, pet supplies or groceries.

Planning Mode

A highly productive mode, planning mode includes the ability to anticipate seasonal needs and product purchases, the visualization of trips and travel, the integration of family scheduling, planning, and gathering, and preparation prior to purchase—among other things. Forty-five percent of consumers were in planning mode yesterday.

Today, consumers go into planning mode while they do other things. In the past, planning mode may have been a mode that required quite a bit of focus. Planning a vacation, for example, likely involved a trip to a storefront travel agency, poring over destination and hotel brochures and advertisements, and phone calls to airlines and hotels to book reservations. Most participants in our study rated planning mode as being more or less like other productive modes, none of which required high levels of focus.

Travefy is an example of a tool that does a pretty good job of helping consumers stay in planning mode. Described as an all-in-one trip planner, it allows you and your friends to plan a trip together and split shared travel costs. Small groups are able to build itineraries together as well as track each others' expenses.

Playing Mode

We anticipate that people will want to play more, be better immersed in play, and have more meaningful connections between or among people through play. No mode has the power to keep the consumer spending more time with you than playing mode.

Although playing mode is more immersive, in terms of focus and pace playing feels to consumers a lot like browsing & exploring. Consumer we studied, most of whom it should be stressed were not gamers, were very open to doing multiple things when in playing mode. They felt that playing should leave them calm and moving at their own pace rather than feeling inspired, enlightened, and surprised – or challenged excessively, for that matter. I am sure that there are variations on this mode that a company that targets playing mode will need to be aware of, but which we did not specifically identify or study. The individual consumer's degree of gaming competitiveness might be one factor affecting the intensity of attention to play versus openness to doing other things while in playing mode.

We need only point to the viral-sensational popularity of games like Angry Birds and Candy Crush to gauge the potentially insatiable appetite among digital consumers to be in playing mode. Although it may be worth noting that for some, such games can easily take on an addictive quality, as study participant April confesses: "Sadly for me, Candy Crush Saga is not 'just a fad,' it is an addiction. I purposely did not load this app on my new phone in order to curb my addiction and expose myself to better uses of my time. I only have it on my laptop now, but I still love to play."

Producing Mode

When consumers are in producing mode they are getting things done. In fact it is when they are most serious about getting things done. In our study therefore, it is not surprising that banking was a key example of being in producing mode. During this mode there is a feeling of task importance and stress that leads to productivity and accomplishment. It is not the best time to sell.

An example of a solution that supports producing mode is Wunderlist. The company is founded on the belief that we need to free our minds of all distractions, no matter how minor. Built on the philosophy of GTD – Getting Things Done –they've integrated the GTD ethos into their product, which at its core is a basic system in which users write down tasks and cross them off as they go. The platform is structured so that users can click onto any number of separate lists (work, private, etc.) and add tasks, subtasks, due dates, reminders, files and notes.

Fifty-three percent of consumers were in producing mode yesterday, and as you might imagine, producing mode features the highest and fastest levels of intensity and pace. Consumers want to get things done. They want to check those boxes off quickly and move on to the next one.

Competing Mode

Americans love to compete on just about every level (though we might presume that people from other nations are really no different in this regard). After all, we took the quintessential non-competitive invention of the peace and love generation Frisbee and turned it into ruthless forms of numerous highly competitive Ultimate Frisbee games including some versions that qualify as a contact sport. Today we have highly popular television shows that feature fiercely competitive dancing, dating, singing and so on. So it is with good reason, I believe, that we may anticipate that digital consumers will be in competing mode with greater frequency in the future. As more of consumers' personal lives become trackable, consumers will want to keep score and improve their score from health and fitness to gaming and everything in between. When we surveyed 1000 consumers, 27 percent said they were in were in competing mode yesterday.

Whether its fitness, gaming, work productivity, or shopping, elements of competition are increasingly becoming a part of the milieu. Consumers actively seek out events where they can compete. Even charitable events feature semi-competitive fundraising events like 5k run/walks or challenges like the recent (and viral) ice bucket challenge for ALS. We anticipate that homes, stores, cars, and cities will be enhanced to allow consumers to engage in this high-energy mode.

The Value of Modes

Companies should design their value propositions to target consumer modes rather than consumer demographics. Modes, as fundamental ways of thinking and behaving that consumers 'get into' that help them get things done, offer a much more potent and powerful insight into who individual consumers are and what they are trying to do or achieve. By targeting one or more modes for your value proposition, you are effectively aligning your goods, services, or experiences with the way that consumers not only go about doing what they want to do when they want to be productive, or when they are planning, or socializing, or browsing & exploring, but in a highly connected world, if successful, you may also be establishing an ongoing presence in their daily course of conduct that enables you to reach the end-goal of helping consumers to complete recurring jobs as a matter of routine.

CHAPTER FIVE

DATA + CONTENT CREATES THE PACKAGE
Context-Aware Content Requires You to Increase the Amount of Data Tied to Content

Lesson 5

Companies that are focused on creating content for distribution should turn their attention to focusing on ways to create the Package. Smart Media companies need to find ways to increase the amount of data that both informs and travels with the content they produce. In Digital Context, consumers will want their content to be "intelligently" informed by different data types. Companies are used to very basic data being embedded in or attached to content. However, context-aware content requires that companies find ways to share data about biometrics, queues, relationships, environments, brands, and other data types, including data that has been analyzed for the benefit of the consumer.

A Thoughtful Package

Imagine that someone designed a package just for you. It was gift wrapped with paper that represents things you like. Inside there's a gift that seems perfect for the moment. You can tell that there was a lot of thought that went into the package and the gift. Now, imagine that it's a different day and a different type of moment. But the package is still perfect for the moment. Wouldn't that be wonderful?

In this chapter I'm going to talk about the relationship between data and content. I'm going to call the smart combination of data types and video, audio, or textual content, the Package. I'm going to suggest to you that if you are in the business of producing content, you really should get into the business of producing the Package. Consumers' expectations for Digital Context will far exceed their expectations for mobility. Content must get smarter while at the same time be sharable and context-aware. I'm going to suggest to you that content producing business models post-Internet of Things will be focused more on key activities associated with data design than on channel distribution. I'm also implying that *every* company can learn about data design by observing what consumers want from rich, context-aware content.

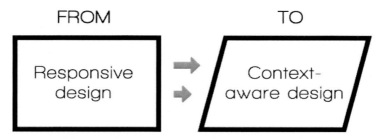

To study data and context, the Collaborative generated five mobile app concepts. Each concept emphasized a different part of Digital Context. For example, M. Sullivan was an app that we created for a fictitious clothing retailer. It was designed to study how consumers would respond to iBeacons within stores that made the environment smart and talked to smart phones. Car Care was a tool that integrated with your car and gave you timely advice about who to go to for car repairs, tracked your motoring activity, and the impact of different brands on consumers' perception of sharing data. Travel Freeze, a feature that helped consumers stay in vacation planning mode, focused on retargeting and modes. Subscription Management, an app we used to explore why people subscribe, is a concept that organizes and manages your subscriptions.

We learned a lot of lessons from the consumers with whom we shared these prototypes. Perhaps the most important lesson for us was: when studying data and solutions, use tools to illustrate the concepts. When you ask consumers in the abstract about their willingness to share data (as we did in quantitative study we discussed in chapter 3) people tend to be 'abstract' in their responses. Their attitudes toward data sharing soften when they see a prototype of a tool they just might like to have. They can imagine better the benefits of sharing data when they are able to realize that by doing so, the tools with which they are sharing that information will both provide options and help them make decisions.

There was another app we conceptualized, called Content Genius. It was designed to help us explore our hypotheses about content and prediction. It, along with the other prototypes, taught me a lot about data, permission, the need to share, and the Package.

The Need to Share Data

August 2015 was a difficult month for some people. They believed they were signing up for a super safe adultery facilitating site, called Ashley Madison. They trusted that they could shop for infidelity the way they shopped for movies—from the privacy of their own computer. Then, on August 18, a group of hackers called Impact Group posted the email addresses, names, and other contact information of millions of people who had frequented the site. There was over 10 gigabytes of information. The news media argued that this breach was unlike any other breach. Here's Caitlyn Dewey's read in the Washington Post, dated August 20.

> In the post-Target, post-Home Depot, post-OPM world, we're no longer shocked or scandalized by even the largest corporate hacks. But we've never seen a breach even half as ruinous or as imminently destructive as the one that just exposed 36 million possible adulterers to a gawking public.
>
> It included full names, birth dates, marital statuses and, perhaps most damningly, intimate details about its users' kinks and sexual preferences — the sort of dirt that, depending on your circumstances, can easily become grounds for firing, divorce, jail time or even execution.
>
> In a few keystrokes, an anonymous, ideologically motivated group managed to torch the careers, friendships and marriages of millions of people. That's not "vandalism," to use a term that Ashley Madison itself has lately resorted to.

That's terror. And it should terrify you.

Later in the article she quotes an authority, "'If understood in more abstract terms,' the Awl's John Herman foretold Tuesday, 'this hack has the potential to alter anyone's relationship with the devices and apps and services they use every day … It's a powerful reminder of the impossibility of perfect privacy.'"

My heart breaks for all of the families that are devastated by the news of a spouse's infidelity. What a cruel and corrupt site! I seem to remember a Bible verse that suggested that in the last days, people's sins would be shouted from rooftops. Sounds like a fulfillment of prophecy. The intensely personal nature of this particular hack coupled with Dewey's commentary regarding the terror that everyone should feel – because we have all shared secrets to some degree with corporate servers – leads to a very important question: will consumers stop sharing data? Will they opt out? Will they withhold?

What's disturbing about the vulnerability that such data breaches expose is that consumers don't have to share data; they need to share data. In order for consumers to accomplish their goals through digital, create immediacy, and respond to smart channels, they must share data; they really have no other choice but to opt out almost entirely. Context Comfortables understand this. I don't know if data breaches like the one that happened at Ashley Madison will curb certain immoral online activities. Perhaps it will. That, frankly, would be a good thing. But consumers will definitely continue to share data. The data they share produces the experiences they want. As Dewey puts it: "The post-Ashley-Madison Internet is a paranoid, disquietous place. But don't worry: You'll get used to it. If you haven't already."

The reason why most consumers will keep sharing data even when there is some risk that their data will be more widely shared without their permission is because the whole purpose of sharing data is to close the gap between thought and action. As I mentioned previously, the promise of digital is to close the gap. Our stay-at-home mom, Heidi had an emotional and social job she needed to get done. She needed to vent about her child's behavior. In order to vent, she must share data because, after all, venting in solitude doesn't do any good. She does so in hopes that she will realize the emotional and social benefits she seeks – the commiseration of other parents in the same situation mostly – faster than she could get if she wrote a family letter about her child.

I remind you of this because I think companies often approach data sharing the wrong way. For most companies the purpose of collecting data is to observe and understand consumer activity. Companies who approach shared consumer data as purely an analytics play are missing the boat. They stop short of the most important things they can learn about their customers' needs and desires.

Companies must begin to see data as a strategic resource on par with human, intellectual, physical, and other resources that are already acknowledged requirements for successfully doing business with their customers. Resources need to be developed, cultivated, and used to produce better product, or better and broader customer support not just interpreted into more targeted advertising campaigns. Multi-platform business model companies often get caught the way Spotify recently did. They change their data collection policies to capture more data from consumers for advertisers, but not for consumers' benefit. This is not the reason that Heidi chose to share more data about herself.
Source: http://www.wsj.com/articles/
spotify-plans-on-customer-data-use-meet-heavyweight-opposition-1440171113

You might think of the data-content dynamic this way. If you've ever watched one of the zillions of crime scene dramas on television or cable, you know how the formula typically proceeds for solving the murder or whatever other heinous crime has been committed.

First, a legion of CSIs descend on the scene with cameras and chemicals and ultraviolet lights and all sorts of other sophisticated investigative equipment, all designed to gather evidence. They take dozens of photographs before they remove anything; they pluck suspected human hairs from the floor or the furniture, dab the unfortunate victim's spilled blood for DNA identification, or "bag" his or her cell phone for the purpose of examining calling activity; they dust doorknobs and computer keyboards for finger prints, and so on. In effect, they strive to collect every possible speck of what we might refer to as "raw data," much of which appears utterly meaningless by itself, but which might prove to be significantly valuable when placed into the context of all of the other evidence gleaned from the crime scene in tow.

Next, all of the evidence, these hundreds of discrete bits of raw data, are sent to the CSI lab where they are extensively and intensively studied and analyzed. Characteristically, it is only after a thorough and painstaking analysis is complete that the investigators are able to meticulously piece together a complete picture of everything that most likely happened at the crime scene, leading of course, to the solution of the crime and the identification and apprehension of the perpetrator.

Well, for our purposes, we might think of that volume of discrete, seemingly unrelated raw data lifted (to use one of those cool CSI terms) from the crime scene analogously as the wealth of information about themselves that digital consumers are willing to share, whether with their tools or with companies. Everything from what they are thinking to what they are doing or working on at the moment, to what they are trying to accomplish in the moment. So that's data.

Now, the thorough and precise analysis of that data "in the lab" (to borrow the metaphor) is what can lead companies (and smart tools) to the successful creation and development of relevant and targeted content that will be of highest interest to consumers and will also be of the most help to them as they are trying to accomplish their goals. So that's content. More importantly, that's the basis for context-aware content.

Thus, data as defined here is essentially anything – any bits of information – that can be identified and tracked about the consumer that can be analyzed and integrated, and which through that analysis can be used to create and build a consumer profile. From that analysis, good, informed content is that which can be most effectively designed to both help the consumer get things done and to improve the digital consumer's overall experience. In this way, to my way of thinking, what we might think of as the universe of clue data contained within a crime scene environment offers an extremely palpable, almost visceral comparison to the universe of data available for tracking within the consumer's digital context, as well as a kind of snapshot of what "context-aware" content should entail; an awareness, if you will, of the whole metaphorical "crime scene" that comprises the consumer's digital context.

With that in mind, it should be clear that companies that are able to see data as a resource to be used for the betterment of the consumer experience will need to design the data experience – that is, through precisely designed content – for the consumer first. This chapter looks at a data design by focusing on one type of company: content providers. However, the principles of design are similar for solution providers.

> Historically, content business models have been built around distribution. Going forward, however, content business models will be built around data design.

Historically, content business models have been built around distribution. Going forward, however, content business models will be built around data design. That is, because of Digital Context, the companies that will be most successful at producing and providing content will be those companies which understand the functional, emotional, social, and aspirational jobs that consumers want to get done with their content, which know how to get the consumer into a mode, and which have permission from the consumer to collect different types of data to improve their ability to affect their field of play.

And data design is very important to content providers. All consumers want content to be customized to them. Let me say that again, slightly differently. All consumers want content customized for their situation and preferably in the moment or mode they are in. When we studied different ways to customized content, we found that No Comfort and Reluctant consumers were sometimes more interested in personalized content than High Comfort consumers. For example, consider the graph on the following page where we asked consumers to tell us what they most or least wanted a smart media player to do for them. Notice that all consumers are already predisposed to receive content that is customized based on past activity. And No Comfort consumers want that type of customization more than High Comfort consumers! While most consumers are not predisposed to see content customized based on their environment, still No Comfort consumers are more likely to want this feature than High Comfort consumers. As the benefits of location, environment, and time of day become more apparent to consumers, you will see lift in these areas as well. All we need to do is look at Spotify to see the positive impact that these types of customizations bring.

Content providers need to create content that is context aware. While data has always been associated with content, context-aware content requires a new order of data sharing. I call this enhanced relationship between data and content, the Package. Content providers need to learn how to produce the Package, a topic we will discuss more in a moment.

Digital Context will bring tools and content that are more predictive. But being predictive has its drawbacks. Digital Context will also bring more queuing and more curating. Striking the right balance between queuing and curating is essential to employing data and content as a strategic resource. I'll share a few of our findings on prediction and curation from 2015.

Before we go deeper into the Package and prediction, let's focus on data types. In 2015, one of the key objectives of the Digital Consumer

Collaborative was to find out what makes consumers want to share more data. What we learned is that the question is too broad. A better question is, "What kind of situations create the right environment for sharing?" The right kind of situation is one in which the consumer, having understood the benefits of sharing, gives permission to the company to access and use different data types.

Data Types and Permission

I am borrowing the term 'data types' from big data thinking. Sunil Soares introduced the concept of big data types to help companies who are analyzing big data using tools like Hadoop. Soare's five types of big data are:

- Web and Social Media (clickstreams, through rates, content, and postings)

- Biometric (facial recognition, genetic, etc.)

- Machine to Machine (sensor data, RFID, GPS)

- Big Transaction Data (health care claims, telecom data, utility records)

- Human Generated (call center voice recordings, email, electronic medical records)

These types of data focus on the volume, velocity, variety and 'value' of the data so that algorithms for accessing and using the data can be developed—a good thing. The only problem with defining data by its bigness is that bigness really doesn't tell you anything about what the consumer wants to do with the data or why the consumer would share that data. Rather than analyze the data collected based on its bigness, our approach categorizes data based on consumers' willingness to allow an exchange and their likelihood to use informed content based on the data they share. More specifically, our approach focuses on the consumer engagement potential of data. To do that we have to focus on permission rather than on bigness.

Through our digital ethnographic studies we've identified eight major data types that consumers regularly give permission to companies to access and to share. They are:

location

- Location: Currently, the most important data type for creating context, location data is used for life logging, navigation, photo tracking, search, or localization to support mobility and immediacy. Consumers give permission readily for location data when they are on the move or when they are setting goals. We found some concern among consumer for sharing location data with family.

biometric

- Biometric: One of the fastest growing categories of data, biometric data is data that tracks movements, heart rate, mood, sugar levels, or other bio data to support health, well-being, and comfort. Today, consumers primarily give permission for biometric data to be shared when they are feeling either bad or good (presumably to help them to "fix" the former or to affirm the latter as a result) about their bodies and when they are focused on goal attainment. In the future, consumers may become much more open to sharing biometric data so that tools and environments can adjust to the types of activities they are involved in. Presently however, they remain most uncomfortable with sharing this data type broadly. A good depiction of this "uneasy willingness," comes from participant Igor D., who clearly sees the future potential of biometric data tracking: "Data I have visibility to that I can use for trending and behavior modification purposes is helpful. That's what fitness trackers and apps do for me and I enjoy creating and analyzing this data.

- I like my fitness and activity being measured and trends created based on those measurements.... I would also allow inter-app sharing and measurement if it was a truly collaborative learning/monitoring experience to support my interests/modes/behaviors. We're not really there yet."

queues

- Queues: Data that tracks activity in key queues such as mail, app usage, payments, calendars, and entertainment can be used to support anticipation of jobs to get done. Queue data speeds up decision-making and thinking. Permission to access or share data is usually given when consumers are in organizing mode or another productivity mode. Companies want queue data for the purpose of providing product and service offers but consumers have concerns about sharing this data for offers. They will share primarily to empower themselves. Study participant Auros H. puts it succinctly when he states that, "Helpful data collection reduces my cognitive load. It makes my work faster. It reduces the effort for, or entirely eliminates, mundane tasks (like tracking a schedule, balancing a budget, getting from point A to B), freeing up my brain to work on more important things."

social

- Social: Social data is different from other queue data because consumers primarily give permission to access or share this data when it helps them to feel connected to friends and family. Social data can be used to support mood, recommend things that friends enjoy, deepen relationships, and reduce loneliness. Consumers have become remarkably comfortable with sharing social data. "I love sharing pictures with family," states Mike G., "I like to share milestones and let people know how I am doing. But I generally only like to share good things. I am not one to vent on social media about the smallest of things." It might be noted that, as evidenced by Heidi earlier, and as even a cursory review of just about any social media portal, like Facebook in particular, unlike Mike there are plenty of people out there who *are* quite willing to share both bad and good things!

tool
productivity

- Tool Productivity: Every tool can or should generate data about its own productivity. Specifically, tool productivity data relates directly to the device or thing that is being used. When consumers grant permission to capture tool productivity data they expect the data to be used to support enhanced capabilities or added features within that device which in turn will help to increase their productivity. They are most likely to give permission for tool productivity data sharing when getting into a mode.

brand

- Brand: Data that tracks the depth and breadth of engagement with a brand and support speed to decision are forms of brand data. Consumers are most likely to give access to and share this data when they are feeling loyal or after a purchase. Brand data will become increasingly important as more products are connected to the Internet of Things and companies can begin to see how a brand is connected to other brands. Keira K.'s comments illustrate just how personal brand data can "feel" to consumers, when she states, "I am willing to share data with a company/brand if the company uses my data to alert me to content that is relevant to me (my purchase history or interests). I'm also willing to share if I have access to certain perks, such as exclusive content or discounts. But, I want to know what data is being collected by the company when I share and I want the ability to opt out if I so desire."

environmental control

- Environment Control: Data that flows through sensors and empowers the consumer to exert control over the environment is environment control data. Most remote security and garage door openers used today are examples of this type of activity. Increasingly, almost all aspects of homes will be connected. Consumers give permission to share or access this data before arrival at the environment or activity if it adds to convenience, control, and comfort.

relationships

- Relationships: Spread out among calendars, emails, phone calls, and texts are data regarding family and friends, activities, preferences, and patterns. This data type will become more prevalent as a wider spectrum of the activities of individuals within a household is tracked. Consumers give permission to access or share this data if the tool supports group dynamics and helps them get social jobs done. This type of data can only be shared when explicit permission is given universally by all parties

involved. Some sociologists and psychologists have even suggested that after the tragedy of 9/11, and in a world where violent
incidents can occur in an instant at any time both at home and
abroad, people are generally more interested (and more comfortable) with simply knowing where their loved ones are and
what they're doing at any given time. Mike G. states, "I find it
incredibly helpful to share location data with family too. We are
all hooked up with Find My Friends on the iPhone, and I'll do
things like check to see if my wife is driving before I text her so I
know she won't be distracted. My wife uses it to see where I am
and how far away from home I am so she knows when to start
dinner. It is kind of neat actually that you can do that IMO."

Data is the lifeblood of Digital Context. If the consumer cuts off
data exchange, he or she will limit what the company can see and do.
Consequently, consumers have a vested interest in data being shared.
Context really began to form first around location data. A consumer's ability to gain content based on his or her location closes the gap between
thinking and doing and empowers the consumer. A company's ability to
share content based on location creates a greater opportunity to engage
the consumer while the consumer is doing something else. Consider
ShopCloud's new Space Tag app, which enables you to tag specific places
and leave eternal notes in "space" for yourself or others, such as a recommendation for a comfortable hotel or a terrific restaurant. When other
travelers, and potential patrons of those establishments, come into proximity to them, your tag and image pop up. Or imagine the potential for
customer and vendor alike if upon arriving at the airport you generally
use for air travel, you are instantly provided with a list of today's specials at
your favorite coffee shop on the terminal concourse, or the latest arrivals at
the bookstore most suitable for reading on the plane, perhaps even tailored
to your specific preferences based on past purchase choices.

A key goal of most companies who develop Digital Context strategies will be to leverage multiple data types to produce experiences. To do so
requires tools and other solutions that perform activities that legitimately

benefit from multiple data types. Later in this chapter, I will look more closely at how content and these data types function together. But let's switch gears here for a minute and talk about smart media channels.

Smart Media Channels Sell Things

There are a lot of ways that data sharing in Digital Context impacts consumer behavior. Let's focus for now on media channels. By a media channel I mean cable and network companies who are now competing against tools like Youtube, Netflix, and Hulu. I am also talking about print providers such as the *New York Times* and *Wall Street Journal* who compete head to head with the online Yahoo! and Huffington Post. So far the debate within and among these companies has been focused on who is gaining more viewerships (once upon a time called "circulation") and the fact that consumers value the tools more than they value the channels. The debate has to date been about value proposition (free and always at your finger tips), revenue (advertising and eyeballs) and customer segments (who prefers traditional channels and who wants digital). The rules of the game were built around the idea that: Content generates interest; interest generates demand; and demand leads to sales. It was essentially an AIDA model that was the foundational basis for media channels.

Today the customer journey is changing. Consumers queue things. They see things they like and they buy. Done. If it's in the queue and they are in the right mode, it's a no brainer. They close the gap between thought and action with a single keytroke. A number of smart media channels are realizing the value of allowing the consumer to purchase directly from their tools. Social media tools like Facebook and Pinterest allow you to purchase directly through their tools. Vine and Youtube, smart media channels, are also allowing direct purchase from their tools. Smart media channels are becoming smarter transactional channels. They no longer conform to the AIDA model. The digital tools you use to interact with these smart media channels are in every sense of the word, queues. Queues provide short cuts for consumer decision-making. A trusted queue is a safe place to press *buy*.

As I've said before, when a smart media channel offers the ability purchase, recommend, share, or produce, the channel is behaving more like a tool and less like a media channel. Digital tools make better smart media channels than media channels do because they close the gap; they help customers to accomplish things quickly and easily. Do you see where I'm going with this? The evolution toward Digital Context will impact media companies in the following ways:

- The pressure that media companies will feel from goods, services, and experience providers will be to create content that does more than attract eyes. It must sell things

- The channels through which companies distribute content will separate into two categories: dumb channels and queues. The queues will function to recommend content and things for sale based on your preferences, situation, and mode

- The number of eyeballs generated does not necessarily equal success. Niche content that is successful in getting consumers into a mode to press 'buy' may be more effective – and much more strategically targeted – than mass content

- Channels really aren't in any sense of the word channels anymore. And companies who see their tools as primarily distribution vehicles are missing the opportunity to be far more integrated into the consumer's life through tools that recommend, guide, suggest, and support the individual, almost like a knowledgeable friend

Channels that become smart tools will be hired by the consumer for the job that they help the consumer to get done. There are millions of functional, emotional, social, and aspirational jobs to get done through content. Some companies will create individual queues within their tools to do different jobs (think Spotify Discover), but other companies will become very proficient in one type of job to get done and will potentially become well known for that proficiency. In either case, as we have already seen, companies will need to focus on recurring jobs to get done so that they remain always in the consumer's queue.

I am not suggesting, however, that media content will be designed specifically for one tool. We know that consumers want content to travel between devices. They want content to travel across tools too, and there may very well be benefits for companies like Netflix to share original content with other companies. What I am suggesting is that content itself must become more meta-data rich so that it can conform to the unique requirements of the tools and environments it is shared in. It must become smarter. Historically, content business models have been built around distribution. Going forward content business models will be built around data design.

When I speak of content, I am talking about both the video/audio/ print content people consume and enjoy as well as the advertising content that is embedded into the experience. Both need to become smarter. One could argue that advertising content is smarter than most long format/ short format video, audio, or print, because advertising content is often served up based on some previously gathered intelligence about things that you've viewed in the past or are interested in—independent of the platform you viewed the content in.

Now, Back to the Package

Let's get back to data types now. One of the key questions we asked ourselves in the 2015 Digital Consumer Collaborative is to attempt to learn what the direction of content will be over the next three years. When we started our research, I truly thought we would be studying whether consumers would want long-format or short-format video and print. What became obvious as we interviewed consumers is that they wanted both and more. What they shared with us is a desire for content that fits their moment, their situation. The only way to deliver a wide range of different types of content that informs, connects, and entertains consumers the way they want to be engaged is through data sharing. Consumers must share data if they want a more customized, anticipatory experience.

Recently I was thinking about Anthony, a consumer from New York, who we met in 2015. Anthony streams video from Amazon Prime, Vudu, Google Play, Netflix, and various channel apps. He watches them on his Ultrabook, laptop, TV, and Android tablet. He said:

> *"All of my TV/movie queues are similar. I am allowed to add, play, pause, resume and remove at will. The Amazon Prime "Resume" feature is not always consistent. This is the same case with my Vudu queue. Sometimes I am able to return to a paused TV episode/ movie at the time at which I paused it and sometimes not. This is*

inconvenient but I would not say that it causes me to become anxious or frustrated. In these types of situations, I always assume that the company will eventually perfect the website's design and the 'glitches' will be eliminated."

Think about the sameness of the video experience across these tools. Granted the content available may be different, but in effect the only thing you can really do with video is play, pause, back up, increase/decrease volume, and stop. It's the digital equivalent of having a VCR.

Content developers should start focusing their data utilization energy on the design of a data-rich content package. The Package is different from what companies are used to designing and producing today. Today you can 'customize' video content by embedding interactivity into the video, for example using WireWAX, which allows you to put product buttons into the video for consumers to click on for immediate purchase. You can also add meta tags. Or you can use APIs like the one for HTML5. Take a look at the properties of the HTML5 media event API properties. They include:

- Volume control
- Width and height control
- Current time
- Duration
- Loop
- Preload
- Buffered
- Played
- Volume

So, in effect, using the API, you can play, pause, and seek in the entire video, change the volume, mute, change the playback rate. You can resize, change volume, and suspend the video. All are great things to be able to do.

Now let's imagine video within Digital Context. There is data sharing going on all around the video. Consumers are sharing bio data, queue data, social data. How, through the API, does the data affect the video content? Currently there is no connection between the video and the data being shared. The API would need to be much more robust to do things like:

- Design the video experience to fit the type of viewing the consumers wants to enjoy. For example, within purges, binging, fast downloads, on whatever screen they have in front of them, is it easy to get back to the last spot if they have to stop watching, etc.
- Queue the right video based on the mood or proclivity of the consumer
- Customize the content of the video based on the time of day
- Inform the video presentation with information about the current location
- Or better, enhance the video experience based on the location
- Time certain content to align with the set up of a product

You can sense that consumers like Anthony would embrace far more contextual insight when he makes comments like, "Netflix is the closest, by far, because they think like the consumer. They know that you are going to purge-watch a series." When you are designing the Package you must be thinking about the uses or features of video or print that go beyond the functional viewing of the content. You are obliged to be thinking about how the content fits within the environment. You are producing both the content and the data experience that together make the content context-aware.

Designing the Package may or may not entail an API. A media company may decide that its approach to serving up content should be maintained within its own tool or tool set. Whether it's an API or not is not the point, however. The question is more strategic: How can a company use contextual data to enhance the content experience? And a second question: how can an enhanced content experience help the company to gain advantages within its field of play?

An enhanced content experience is something that No Comfort consumers want as much or more than High Comfort consumers. Think about that. In our research we found that No Comfort consumers were more concerned about how to find videos than High Comfort consumers. No Comfort consumers need a well crafted Package just as much as anyone else.

Designing the Package is a strategic act. A content provider should be asking themselves:

- What modes does this Package support
- What data types does this Package require in order to deliver the experience our customers/consumers want
- How do we know when an appropriate moment for the content is forming
- How do we orchestrate activity across different Packages
- How do we use the data shared to discover new opportunities and new jobs to get done

With a better understanding of data types and modes, companies can serve content or shape content to better fit the consumer's situation. Whether the content is educational/informational, entertainment, or content created to produce a communicative connection between people, the product is better if analytics are used to capture how consumers consume content in different modes and how different data types can be combined and used to enhance the experience.

Different Data Types and Different Content

This year we put our big toes into the pool of designing the Package by asking consumers what came to mind when they thought about content and different data types. I say dipped our big toes in because I mean just that. There is so much more to study regarding how data types affect content. Let me share some examples of things we explored.

Biometric Data and Content

We asked participants in our study to use three different tools: Spark People, Fitbit, and My Fitness Pal. Then we asked them to brainstorm ideas for how to improve the content of these tools based on these categories: health, diet, skill, goals, and comfort/lifestyle. Here's one consumer's responses to how to improve My Fitness Pal. She said,

- Health: I would like to be able to share my information across all of my health apps

- Diet: I wish there was a scan option – where I could scan a bar code and it would enter or match the info. That would make my life easier – it gets tedious entering things manually that aren't there, and I give up. Rewards for eating properly during the day

- Skill: Keep me on course or on track. Educate me and strengthen my health skills

- Goals: I really wish it would alert, or buzz, or SOMETHING when I forget to log in. It's too easy to just not do it, and I wish they would fix that

- Comfort/Lifestyle: Set up a food or diet challenge for me based around proper diet and exercise routine. When I travel help me to have food choices that are set to my geographic location

Notice how her responses indicate that she immediately sees the advantages of different data types being combined with biometric data to improve the content experience. She *wants* My Fitness Pal to know where she is and to combine that data with other data about her approach to diet, which poses a very customized challenge to the tool. She wants the tool to function more effectively as a queue, alerting her when she forgets to log in. She sees the content that will be produced from combining biometric, queue, and location data as being of greater, more wide-ranging benefit to her.

You can see how much more dynamic her vision of content in My Fitness Pal is than what we typically think of when we are considering content. It's not hard to imagine content being produced and displayed by My

Fitness Pal that also adjusts to mood, food intake, family dynamics, etc. She is giving the tool permission to understand her. She also wants the tool to share what it knows with other tools to make them better.

My Fitness Pal is a great tool to study because it implies tracking of activity. The Package that media companies create most likely needs to track the consumer. Now, think about Comcast's cable service. Comcast has a hidden fitness program called Comcast Exercise Television. It's buried in the middle of Comcast's On Demand feature. It would be easier for the app to start a content channel related to fitness than it would be for the behemoth cable provider to design a Package that consumers value. My Fitness Pal is better positioned than Comcast to deliver the experience that consumers' want from media because of the data it collects about the consumer. Fitness apps have permission to collect biometric data. Cable channels don't.

Location Data and Content

We asked consumers to think about location data and content by doing a similar exercise. They used four different tools: YELP, Urban Spoon, iBotta, and Instagram. We then asked them to think about how location data could make these experiences better. We identified specific locations or environments to focus on: in store, at home, in a car, in a hotel, and at work. Here's what three of our participants came up with for YELP:

- In store: Better way to filter Reviews based on my location. Working on giving better directions to desired business

- At home: Match me to restaurant diners that write reviews and have similar tastes as me

- In car: Better use of GPS to help locate the business when traveling to look for the business's location

- In a Hotel: This app may be able to list the amenities of the hotel

- At work: Sync with my other like apps for ease and convenience, to allow them to be more productive

When I look at these responses the thing that jumps out at me is how much we take location tracking for granted today. We used to make a big fuss over having our location tracked. Now, most consumers see the benefit. Content that isn't location aware just isn't smart enough anymore. Content providers should be filtering things based on the environment in which the content is consumed. YELP makes recommendations, so naturally, we expect it to make more specific recommendations based on location data. When we think about a smart media channel we are less inclined to think that it is a recommendation tool. But that is exactly what it is. I think you could take these three consumers and ask them to do a similar exercise for YouTube. Their ideas would be very similar. Location data today means better recommendations. It means the ability to accomplish your goals. It celebrates the place and suggests the journey forward (e.g., Space Tag again). Media should celebrate the location. We need more video and print content that adapts to the location and encourages the consumer to enjoy where they are at or where they are going.

Social Data and Content

Let's do one more data type. Social data is different from other queue data because consumers primarily give permission to access or share this data when it helps them to feel connected to friends and family. We asked our participants to use the following tools: Facebook, Pinterest, Instagram, and Next Door. We then asked them to give us ideas for how to improve the textual content, the video content, and other forms of content. I'm going to share with you some of the responses from participants regarding improvements to textual content.

- For Facebook: They should have options on the newsfeed to filter posts via categories such as Videos, Pictures, Statuses, etc. That way if I only want to read articles or view text that people post, I can more readily view the ones that have been posted instead of having to sort through and scroll through the rest of the newsfeed to find them. Have a better filter for push notifications.

Allow your daily notifications to change in accordance to your mood or how you're feeling on that day

- For Pinterest: I think that Pinterest does a great job with serving up content to me that will interest me based upon the data I've provided. When I type words into the search engine, it suggests posts/pins based upon those direct keywords. I can then 'x' out of a keyword to delete it quickly to altar the search in any way I'd like

- For Instagram: Allow me to go to settings and set up a profile for the type of suggested followers. Talk to text app might be nice for searching out potential people to follow

- For Next Door: Would be good to have settings like busy, working, etc., like instant messaging programs have so you can indicate when you are online and also to see when others are online

Now pay attention to what these participants are saying. To improve the textual content experience in these tools the companies should know more about what's in their queues ("filter posts via categories"), their location (Next Door was valued because it knew social and location data: "would be good for settings like busy, working, etc."), and biometric data ("would be nice if they knew what mood you are in.") Do you see that? The experience gets better when more data types are combined. Content becomes richer and more meaningful.

I started this section by sharing some of the API attributes for video in HTML5. Hopefully, you are now seeing that an API or a tool designed to produce content for Digital Context needs to do so much more than signal start, stop, and rewind. When a company begins to produce content that is data-type aware and mode-aware, that company will be in a very different position of differentiation. That company will be producing the Package.

Anticipation and Curation

Let's say you are working on the context-aware version of Netflix. You've partnered with Fitbit or Apple Watch and gained access to a trove of biometric data. You've partnered with Facebook or Apple Watch and gained access to a trove of social data. You've partnered with Google Now or Apple Watch and have gained bunches of data on location and queues, and environment controls. (You get my point). And now you want to produce a new experience. You are going to know a lot.

You might even think that you can anticipate exactly what movies the consumer will want in a given situation.

Don't.

Just because you can anticipate what a consumer is likely to want doesn't mean you should serve up just that content. There are two reasons for this:

1. Consumers won't like it.

2. All predictive algorithms are based on Bayesian models. But people don't want to always have a Bayesian algorithm telling them what they should do.

During the spring of 2015, the Collaborative conducted co-creation sessions (we call them framing sessions) with consumers. We developed a few basic prototypes to explore the preferences of consumers for different types of content. The primary tool that we invented to study content was Content Genius. It is a recommendation tool that takes into consideration how much time you have and what you are in the mood for and then serves you up a recommended video clip—either from social media sites or from content provided by media companies. The tool has a set up feature that asks questions about modes, device preferences, location, and other filters. Then, through data gathering, the tool gathers insights into the consumer's situation and, when accessed, makes recommendations of video clips that the individual might enjoy.

We asked consumers to do a warm up exercise before discussing the tool where they rated different content providers based on: (A) 'Does not give me what I want' versus 'It's creepy', and (B) 'It makes recommendations based solely on my last choice' versus 'It makes recommendations based on what other people like'. We wanted to understand how these consumers thought about predictive tools for content. The warm up exercise got them talking. The prototype helped them understand what potential existed for content and predictions. And then they started talking and reshaping the prototype.

Harold told a story about his experience with Amazon. He had gone through a period where he loved British spy novels. They were all he read for six months. After that time, however, he got tired of the genre. He wanted something new. But what did Amazon recommend? Spy novels. He said, "I had to train Amazon to show me other things by clicking on them. It took a long time." Harold was experiencing the downside of Bayesian prediction tools. Bayesian inference is the most powerful, perhaps the only real predictive statistical model for assessing the likelihood that something is going to happen. I am not a mathematician. But even I get why the Bayesian theorem is so widely used. It works, as long as you are sure that you have the proper antecedents. A Bayesian mathematical model uses past actions to predict future behavior. Harold had told Amazon that he valued British spy novels. And so Amazon got really good at giving him exactly what his history suggested he'd want.

Sarah thought about the same issue and then began to talk about her concerns. "If an app does too good of a job of predicting what I want," she said, "then I know that I'm missing out on something else that I really don't know about." Sarah gave voice to a concern that a lot of us have. Is the tool showing us only the things that it thinks we are going to want? What are we then missing out on? Content Genius can't be too much of a genius or the consumer begins to feel pigeon-holed and even trapped. You can over-predict what people will want. This principle doesn't just apply to serving up videos. It applies to all aspects of Digital Context.

We want our environments and our tools to anticipate what we might want but we also want to discover on our own. We love to explore and try new things. Jeff said, "I want to see a random Reddit post that would otherwise be overlooked in the mass of information." For this reason perhaps more than any other, consumers will continue to choose a variety of content providers. They like the randomness of certain tools, the consistency of others. They are choosing content based less on their demographics and lifestyle and more based on what the moment seems right for. (Think jobs to get done and modes).

The most successful music tools curate. Curating is a powerful compliment to Bayesian predictions. In certain modes you are going to want more curation (I know, 'curation' is a neologism in the context used here. But go with me on it). Curation creates that experience of guided discovery, of knowing that someone out there has seen something that you wouldn't have seen. It puts the human back into prediction, as in, "I'll bet you're going to like this." In the Internet of Things, where so many machines are talking to each other, it's nice to know that a person was hand picking some of the things that you experienced.

The lesson I have been articulating in this chapter is that companies focused on creating content for distribution should turn their attention to ways to create what I have called the Package, which I have likened to a gift that is perfect no matter when it arrives. What that means briefly stated is that content must be tailored to the individual consumer. Companies that see data as a resource to be used for the betterment of the consumer experience will understand the need to *design* the data experience for the consumer first. Content producing business models post-Internet of Things will be focused more on key activities associated with data design than on channel distribution.

Our research has enabled us to identify eight data types that speak to the functional, emotional, social, and aspirational jobs that consumers want to get done. But more importantly, our studies clearly indicate that consumers readily see the advantages of combining these different data types to create highly customized tools to help them when they get into modes, and they see the content that will be produced from combining location, biometric, queue, relationship, environment, brands and other data types as being of greater, more wide-ranging benefit to them.

Companies that develop a better understanding of data types and modes will be better positioned to serve content or shape content to better fit the consumer's situation, needs and desires. Whether the content is educational/informational, entertainment, or content created to produce a communicative connection between people, the product is better if analytics are used to capture how consumers consume content in different modes and how data types can be used to enhance the experience.

CHAPTER SIX

DON'T FOCUS ON LOYALTY; FOCUS ON POSITIVE ENGAGEMENT

Your Brand Promises Happiness;
Your Experience Needs to Deliver it

Lesson 6

The promise of Digital Context cannot just be to speed things up. Context must improve the wellbeing of people. There is so much research that is currently going on in positive psychology that helps companies think about delivering happiness to consumers. Digital Context should tap into that body of research. On the other hand, companies cannot create context without a return on their investment. Their return will come from ongoing, positive engagement with consumers. This chapter explores why a loyalty mindset is wrong for Digital Context and why a positive engagement mindset is what companies need to go after.

Your Brand Promises Happiness

We all recognize that there is a downside to queues and context. It's not just that people can be overwhelmed by the amount of digital activity that is going on, it's that the effects of digital activity can diminish your health, personal wellbeing, and family life. It is not enough to simply speed things up for consumers. You must take care of them.

Queues create intimate circles in consumer decision-making. They allow consumers to meander while making progress toward multiple goals. However, just as the first queue, the email in-box, quickly became a nonproductive environment because of spam, so also can most other queues.

An increased number of queues alerting consumers to content or tools that have no relevance to the given situation the customer happens to be in will only frustrate people. Tools that use milestones to measure goal attainment can quickly become coercive. Health advocates are rightly concerned about the net effect of digital on people's wellbeing. Some argue that consumers need to separate themselves from all things digital in order to restore balance or peace of mind. There certainly is a need to turn things off sometimes.

Perhaps it wouldn't be your responsibility to take care of the consumer if you were a business that didn't imply that you were customer-centric. But you are. Most consumer-facing companies today promise to make their customers happier. Digital Context can make consumers happier. But it also can make them miserable. Any company that promises happiness and then delivers a miserable experience risks its reputation, destroys its value proposition, and alienates its customers. In the world of Digital Context, making consumers miserable also means you get turned off, perhaps indefinitely.

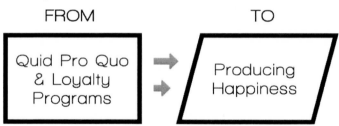

Mary Putman is Vice President of Digital Innovation and Business Development at Hallmark. She's been a part of the Collaborative since its inception. Here's her take on positive engagement.

In thinking about business models, business strategy and data design, we would be better off thinking about people instead of 'consumers.' The labels of consumer, user and shopper are reductive and imply a filter of what is best for the company first. I'm not saying that profits don't matter. They are critical as companies can't survive without them, but the strongest value propositions and business models are based in positive engagement that leads to the loyalty of people—not consumers. Success comes first from really solving problems or adding joy for people so they trust you as a partner and buy why you do things as well as what you do. Understanding jobs and modes comes from walking in her shoes as a person and not just the part of her that consumes, uses or shops. Value propositions and data design should start with what's in it for her. Why would she care? How is it better than what she does to day? Will she understand the benefits?

I stand reprimanded. Indeed we should be talking about people.

Consumption is only a part of who we are. I think the positive psychology movement gets this. You can spend a lot of time designing apps, devices, environments, and content for your context-aware customer experience. However, if your business model is designed to leverage context in ways that damage the wellbeing of people, then your designs will fall apart. Brand strategists have a vested interest in Digital Context because the technology can both engage the consumer and deliver on the promise of the brand. Or not. So, I'd like to start this chapter by sharing a framework that I developed for Stone Mantel and that we've shared with our clients for several years. It's called the Promise Making/Promise Keeping framework.

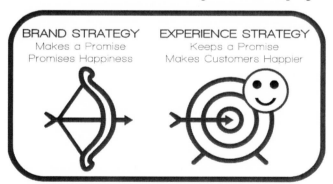

Innovations in brand strategy almost always yield a new promise of customer happiness. This promise takes different forms. Over the years, companies have focused on a wide range of different strategies for promising happiness, including (but not limited to) the promise of exclusive membership within a group of like-minded, cool individuals, or promising that the purchase of a certain product is based on shared values, or promising that a product will bring personal satisfaction. During the recession of 2008-2009, brand strategy evolved—as it always does during recessions—to direct appeals to customer happiness. Think of Coca-Cola's campaign, "Open Happiness." Or Best Buy's tagline, "You, happier." In fact, many companies today are very direct about asserting the fact that when you choose them, they will improve your wellbeing.

Innovations in experience strategy, done right, should help the company keep a promise. Whether it's delivering on customer journey, innovating around jobs consumers want to get done, or managing customer relationship systems, experience strategy is about producing time enjoyably well spent with a company for the customer. Because companies are promising they will make their customers happier, they need to actually deliver happier customers. And Digital Context can help with that—if companies approach context with the right mindset.

A Loyalty Program is the Wrong Mindset

Before we jump into talking about the right mindset, let's talk about the wrong mindset for engaging consumers through IoT. Loyalty models were designed to get customers to return and purchase again. Repurchase remains a very important part of most business models today. And I'm certainly in favor of creating feelings of loyalty in consumers. But how important is returning to the channel if the channel is always with you? The advent of queuing and the increasing prevalence of Digital Context call into question a fundamental premise of all loyalty models: that you need to get the consumer to return. Going forward, it's more important that the customer wants to *turn on* your capabilities and thereafter *leave them on.*

Of course, you want your customers to be loyal. We all do. The problem is that the strategies developed to create loyal customers do not actually make them loyal, they make them return to purchase again. In fact, if you look up the definition of customer loyalty you'll get something like this:

The likelihood of previous customers to continue to buy from a specific organization. Great attention is given to marketing and customer service to retain current customers by increasing their customer loyalty. Organizations employ loyalty programs which reward customers for repeat business.

To me, a loyal customer is someone who willingly continues to *engage* with your company because they like hiring you to get jobs done for them. Whether the job is functional, emotional, social, or aspirational, you need to be the very best at getting the job done on a recurring basis. That's what generates the feelings of loyalty that cause consumers to prefer you. And loyalty should be a result, not a program, for the following reasons:

1. Companies who overly focus on loyalty tend to innovate with an emphasis on customer satisfaction and incremental change. Loyalty has become synonymous with loyalty and rewards programs and Net Promoter Scores. These tactical activities can help you with basic breakdowns in customer experience but cannot help you produce happier customers. If the experience is driven primarily by Net Promoter Scores, the company will often lose its focus on creating a more meaningful experience.

2. Companies who see Digital Context through the lens of a loyalty program will see data as the currency of loyalty. It's not. It's the lifeblood of context. I'll share more about the downside of treating data as currency later. For now, suffice it to say that it's the wrong mindset to bring to a key resource.

3. For the consumer, everything begins to feel like a trap. Customer trust goes down, not up, when companies employ loyalty program tactics to trigger return activity.

Think for a moment about the potential for problems for consumers if most companies employ Digital Context to generate loyalty using today's techniques. What if you have over 20 billion devices connected to the Internet of Things and all of them are focused on getting consumers to return and purchase? That's going to be a horrible experience and the result will be distrust on the part of consumers.

When the Digital Consumer Collaborative started studying data, we didn't intend to study data and loyalty programs. We put together a series of interview activities in which we asked participants questions like:

- What do you want technology to do for you? What do want to specify/control on your own

- What makes you want to share data with a company/brand

- What is the difference between data gathered that is helpful and data gathered that is creepy

- What data about you that could be collected by these companies do you want to see for yourself? Would you like to compare your data with data from other people like you?

- What about yourself do you like being measured? What don't you like being measured

- What data do you want to share with friends or family

What we found is that the more we probed around about how to get consumers to share data with companies, the more they went into '*quid pro quo*' mode. "What's in it for me?" they would ask. And the more they saw data sharing as a *quid pro quo*, the more they assumed all of premises and prejudices of loyalty programs. They saw sharing as analogous to becoming a member of a mileage program. They saw the tracking of data by companies as being something that they should be rewarded for. And most importantly they became suspicious of the ultimate intent of the perceived loyalty program.

When we mentioned the names of specific companies during these activities, consumers immediately became suspicious of each company's intent. The loyalty program mindset killed the consumer's trust of the brand's intentions with respect to gathering data. So, if you want to kill brand trust, turn your data sharing activities into a part of your loyalty program. Done!

Extrapolating from that experience and thinking about how a company's mindset can get in the way of the wellbeing of customers, here's what applying a loyalty program mindset to Digital Context would lead to:

- "Retention" becomes synonymous with "sticky"
- Buying data on consumer purchase habits becomes more important than reputation
- Customer service is about reward programs for the consumer
- The key measure of success is still Net Promoter
- Trust becomes "'we haven't had a data breach'"
- Profiles of target audiences focus on purchase history
- Environments (home, store, car) become promotion traps

Conversely, a wellbeing mindset that employs Digital Context to deliver on promised happiness is likely to result in the following:

- "Retention" means being integrated into the life of the consumer
- Doing jobs for consumers that recur is more important than word of mouth
- Customer service is enhanced by intentional data design
- The key measure of success is engagement
- Trust is built as brands become reliable producers of holistic solutions
- Profiles of target audiences focus on modes, queues, and data types
- Environments (home, store, car) become places that improve people's lives

Moving to Positive Engagement

To deliver happiness to consumers most companies should move from a loyalty program mindset to a customer happiness business model. If you're promising happiness, use Digital Context to deliver happiness. The impact on your business could be transformative.

	Positive Engagement	*Loyalty*
Business Objective	Improve the well be-ing of the customer	Keep the customer as long as possible
Effect	Extrinsic or intrinsic goal achievement	Satisfaction with a product
Strategy	Align business model with experiences that deliver on promises	Respond to incremental needs
Success Metrics	**Engagement, Happiness, Time Well Spent, Goal Achieve-ment**	Recommend, Use, Stay

A focus on customer happiness can transform a company's vision and approach to customer relations, value proposition design, key activities, customer journey, and revenue stream, as well as elevate the company's game and give purpose to its digital strategy. My colleague, Bryan Searing, recently worked with a financial institution to help them deliver on the promises of happiness that their brand was making. He said that the process of helping a company transform and move toward positive engagement was exhilarating for everyone involved. It's so exciting. So let's jump in and explore how you might go about doing just that!

> At almost the exact same time the modern digital world was emerging psychologists were developing insights into how to positively influence human wellbeing.

At almost the exact same time the modern digital world was emerging psychologists were developing insights into how to positively influence human wellbeing. That body of research is now known as positive psychology. Over the past few years the thinking of those who research happiness/positive psychology and digital have begun to overlap. Because positive psychology focuses on helping people live fulfilled, productive lives through an understanding of body, mind, and environment, the role of digital in general, and Digital Context in particular, should be a part of what psychologists study. Technologists are also taking note.

Rafael Calvo and Dorian Peters edited an important, somewhat academic work on the convergence between happiness research and technology, called *Positive Computing: Technology for Wellbeing and Human Potential*. The book covers topics like helping people move toward and maintain a new 'set point' for happiness, what technology can do to emulate empathy, how to approach motivation, engagement, and flow. Each of the chapters is written by psychologists, academics, and technologists who think about the implications of things like whether or not video games positively influence self-esteem (Jane McCoginal says 'yes') or how to embody altruism into virtual reality technologies (Rosenberg, Baughman, & Bailenson show that flying like a superhero makes you more likely to help someone in need). I bet you didn't know that.

My point in discussing the book, *Positive Computing*, is to illustrate that there are a lot of new ways of approaching digital that have the potential to allow you to make a promise and keep it. Through precision design of digital experiences you may actually be able to reduce the stress your customers feel during a commute to work or help them to improve their financial wellbeing. And through Digital Context you may be able to have an even more positive impact than you might have previously imagined. I remember talking to Chris, a Boston resident, who described the notion of positive computing this way.

"I am a lot more productive when the end result/benefit is clear to me. I like to have a target or incentive to shoot for. I need to have that purpose. This ties to happiness. Achieving a goal or incentive gives me a sense of accomplishment. I think when technology is able to tie tasks to goals and create motivation or clarity of a goal or track progress towards it, it helps a lot."

While companies are often surprised that consumers will allow their data to be used to show progress toward a goal, consumers aren't. They want technology to help them progress. At the same time, they don't want technology that makes them feel like they are running on the 'hedonic treadmill.' The hedonic treadmill is the phenomenon of accumulating more without experiencing an increase in happiness. You can imagine all of the new tools created for Digital Context tracking the progress of consumers and telling them exactly what they are doing but in no way increasing their level of happiness. That can't happen.

There are things that companies can do—at a business strategy level—to produce happier customers. I'm choosing my words carefully here. Recently Apple's CEO had harsh words for how Google and Facebook monetize the data they collect The fight between Apple and Google about 'you, the product' should take on a new level of meaning. Specifically, Tim Cook raised the old adage that if the product is free, then you (consumers) are the product. He promised never to monetize people's data for advertising purposes. He can say that because of his company's business model.

Google and Facebook are multi-platform business models that depend on advertising.

But the consumer *could* be the product and still be better off for it if the company used data to produce happiness. That's what medical professionals do. Or yoga masters and fitness coaches, which abound today. A business model based on producing happier customers gives purpose and intent to data collection. If companies want to engage consumers at the level of intimacy that mobility and context provide, then they need to use data, content, and tools to measurably improve the wellbeing of the individual or family or group.

The Business Requirements to Deliver Happiness

I started studying happiness research about seven years ago—before the Digital Consumer Collaborative was launched. The framework I am going to share with you I have written about elsewhere. Based on a survey of literature that started with Socrates, I grouped ancient and modern philosophers and scientists who had studied happiness based on two criteria: first, how they saw the 'aim' of happiness (was it to fulfill a higher purpose or for a sensory experience?) and second, how they saw where happiness is located (is it driven primarily from within the individual or is it a product of the activities of a group/others?), which I called the locus of happiness. These categories grew out of the examination of the literature. Then, I looked at what things needed to be present in an experience to deliver the type of happiness the scholars were describing. Regardless of whether the experience is digital or not, there are requirements that an experience must meet in order to deliver happiness. Positive engagement is an outcome of creating experiences that masterfully deliver on these requirements.

A Transformative Happiness Engagement Model

Many companies promise to transform individuals or organizations. FitBit, Archer Daniels Midland, Nike, SunTrust Banks, MapMyRun, SAP, Weightwatchers—any brand that promises to help you progress from your current state toward a goal is promising a transformative experience.

Whether or not the promise is delivered on depends in large part on the company's ability to execute around five things:

Transformative

1. Goal Attainment. There must be an explicit or implicit goal the consumer is trying to attain.

2. Current State Review. The experience must provide a diagnostic that allows the individual to understand his or her current state.

3. Guides. The experience requires some form of guidance, whether that be from people or tools.

4. New Knowledge. By progressing through the experience, the consumer should gain new knowledge.

5. Flow. During the experience there should be moments when the consumer feels propelled forward or pushed in a positive way to accomplish his or her goals in a way that is challenging.

When these things are present, the company can say that it is delivering an experience that produces transformative happiness. If your brand promises transformation, but your business model can't deliver these things, then you are being false and misleading.

Let's use an example to illustrate how one company's engagement model might produce happier customers. Recently, Under Armour purchased MyFitnessPal and Endomondo. Under Armour's Chief Executive Officer, Kevin Plank, is intent on turning Under Armour into a technology company focused on fitness. Notice, that he did not buy devices. There are no Fitbit-like purchases that he made. The company's focus is on purchasing nutrition and exercise data and then employing that data to improve the wellbeing of consumers through personal transformation. Under Armour recently created a partnership with NBC's newly formed group, Radius, which is NBC's new media channel for fitness content.

Plank has discussed openly his plan to design apparel that monitors your performance. Clearly Under Armour is intent on becoming a brand that promises more transformation than ever before. Under Armour needs to think about ways in which content, data, and technologies will interact within its field of play. Let's think about the different fields of play that Under Armour could be focused on:

- Active Living: Home and local areas for exercise and nutrition

- Travel Journey: Business travel and vacation activities

- Sports: Youth sports or adult sport activities

Within each of these fields of play there are potential partners and competitors. The fields are constantly evolving and Under Armour needs to stay relevant across tools. To do so Under Armour might create three new queues (remember, queues are smart channels) that cross their growing app network and contain content from NBC, Radius, and other partners. The queues should be tied to recurring jobs that consumers want to get done. I would suggest:

- Nutrition: a platform for tracking and managing food intake. Permissions given by consumers to manage location, biometric, brand, and social data belong in this queue. It should also connect to the exercise queue

- Exercise: a platform for tracking and recommending activities that will increase performance. Permissions given from consumers to manage data from the nutrition queue—as well as location, biometric, brand, social, and relationship data

- Advice: a platform with customized, authoritative content for individuals. Permissions given by consumers to track activity on both the nutrition and exercise queues allow you to deliver content recommendations that fit time, location, and interest

You get a sense for what Under Armour might be planning to do from the interview Plank recently gave to CNBC in which he first announced his company's new fitness-based partnership with NBC. "I'm proud of the fact that a piece of apparel and a pair of shoes can help you, but it's good to have a trainer yelling at you every now and then," he said. Can you imagine if the Advice queue contained customized content from Stephan Curry or Tom Brady yelling at you to get your sorry self in shape?

Now that we've got the basic tools to start delivering on transformative happiness, we need to go farther. To deliver on that promise and keep consumers engaged, Under Armour could do the following:

Target modes that support transformational journeys
Be explicit about the fact that Under Armour is taking the individual on a journey. Study what modes consumers are most likely to be in when they start a transformational journey. Design that customer journey to ensure that goal attainment, current state review, guides, knowledge, and flow are well represented. For the sake of this discussion, let's suggest the following:

- Rest and recovery mode
- Warm up mode
- Practicing mode
- Competing mode

Develop key resources, activities, and partnerships that support transformative modes
Under Armour understands the importance of data. Otherwise they wouldn't have purchased MyFitnessPal and Endomondo. The way that any company deploys key resources, especially shared data, should make your organization smarter at designing diagnostics, gathering data that guides people, streamlining and developing flow, and discovering new goals that elevate. Under Armour should be looking to create competitive advantages

through partnerships around the modes that their consumers are likely to be in while they are being transformed.

Create metrics that align with transformation

- When any company delivers transformations, it should measure customer happiness (not satisfaction) using a from/to protocol. Success metrics might include the following:
- Did the individual achieve his or her goals
- Did goal achievement produce a happier customer
- How has the wellbeing of the consumer improved
- What barriers in the journey or modes reduced the effectiveness of the transformation
- How many recurring jobs did the consumers engage in

When Under Armour begins to look at the financial performance of the experiences it creates, it should consider things like:

- The value of the data collected to produce transformation and the impact of that value on the success of partners
- The market size for key modes that it targets
- The ratio of solutions with a subscription to items sold

An Altruistic Happiness Engagement Model

If your brand promises to help individuals to connect with each other, then you are predisposing your customers to expect altruistic experiences. An altruistic experience requires that the following things are present:

Altruistic

1. A common cause. People who participate must have a common purpose for sharing what feels collectively like a meaningful pursuit.

2. Personal preparation. Individuals who participate should be able to contribute something of their own creation to others.

3. A facilitated encounter. A platform for bringing individuals together is provided and should facilitate ongoing activity.

4. Gift giving. The exchange of ideas or things should feel like a gift and not like a transaction.

5. Reconnection. People have the ability to reconnect and want to reconnect on a regular basis.

All social media sites promise, and often deliver, altruistic happiness, although sometimes the ways that social sites monetize through advertising negatively impacts the feelings of a common cause or giving/receiving a good gift. Companies who deploy broad altruistic models are somewhat constrained regarding their revenue models. People assume that sharing should be 'priceless'—literally without price. When you give a gift, you don't want the gift to be price-valued by the receiver. You want the gift to feel freely given, and accepted in that paradigm spirit of "it's the thought that counts." Facebook, Instagram, and most other social sites would struggle to charge a subscription fee in part because it goes against consumer sentiment for gift giving. (And, yes of course, it's also because people like free content). Consequently, there must be a second audience that is willing to fund the exchange. Revenue may come from the two primary segments if the common cause is very compelling and very unique. Broad common causes are almost always likely to result in an advertising or product placement revenue model.

Airbnb is a travel provider that has the potential to create altruistic happiness. As a platform for vacation or travel rental homes and apartments, these companies are in the business of connecting givers (home owners) with receivers (travelers). These companies can use the engagement patterns of altruistic happiness to enhance the customer experience and improve wellbeing. Let's look at how Digital Context thinking and altruistic happiness requirements might change the way they do business.

Recently Airbnb announced two new initiatives: a partnership with Nest Learning Thermostats to help the home-owner hosts conserve energy, and a new platform for "Local Experiences" through which travelers can look for day activities provided by local travel groups. You can sign up for hikes in the woods near San Francisco led by a local guide, or sailing in the Bay with a seasoned mariner. These two initiatives indicate two key fields of play for Airbnb: the host's rental location and the local activity scene surrounding or in close proximity to the property. You can intuitively imagine why Airbnb would want to partner with Nest and in-home IoT-enabled products. They want to better understand how the homes are utilized so that they can make recommendations to hosts to improve the guest experience, (while also improving cost efficiency for the home-owner hosts). In effect, they are likely to use the data to make the 'gift' of the home experience that much more meaningful to travel guests.

For the purposes of this discussion, though, lets focus on their Local Experiences platform. Airbnb Experiences creates a giver and receiver network of local activities. This field of play is ripe for Altruistic Engagement.

What I like about their current version is the way that local activities high-light the individual who leads them. For $25 you can hire Jay, a local, to take you on a tour of Victorian homes in San Francisco. As the tour guide describes it, here's what you get:

> *Tour Pacific Heights with its colorful Victorian row houses, famous mansions, and beautiful gardens. Visit the inside of a period Queen Anne Victorian. See where Ms. Doubtfire and Princess Diaries were filmed, or where Bill Cosby and Francis Ford Coppola lived. The walk is easy and there are no hills to climb.*

> *You'll walk past beautifully manicured gardens in Pacific Heights and enjoy spectacular views of San Francisco Bay including Golden Gate Bridge and Alcatraz. In addition, you'll learn to appreciate the difference between Queen Anne, Italianate, and Stick-Style Victorian architecture.*

Sounds like a great time. Now, how can Airbnb produce happier customers using an Altruistic model? The fact that you have individuals who have prepared these tours, with names like Ryan, Jay, Michael, Nicki, and Alexandra, suggests that there has been intentionally targeted personal preparation, a key engagement requirement, by the tour guides in creating and orchestrating these tours. They are giving something of themselves. It's now Airbnb's job, as a platform provider, to enhance their abilities to give good gifts. Let's conjecture that Airbnb might collect information about their traveler's preferences. In turn, they should share relevant information with the tour guides and suggest opportunities for the guides to customize their tours based on what they know about the group of travelers. They should encourage reciprocity from the travelers. From the other side of this equation, imagine if the travelers could do more than offer up good recom-mendations for the individual tours. What if they could provide the tour guides with step-by-step data regarding the experience that included key junctures at which the tour became most meaningful for them? That would help the tour guides get better and better, honing their product to enhance happiness, while at the same time enabling everyone to feel an even greater sense of attachment to their common cause.

Speaking of common causes, Airbnb should understand what consumers are looking for from a local experience and turn that information into new opportunities for tour guides to explore. Here's a few ideas for common causes:

- The balance of nature and urbanism
- Protecting historic architecture
- Culture and local food
- Getting away, totally
- Friendships from around the world
- Hidden gems

What makes a common cause exciting is when a group of people believe in it. Presently it seems, Airbnb's current iteration of Local Experiences doesn't do a very good job of creating belief in the tours' causes. It mostly treats the tours as a rather passive list of discrete activities. To deliver more happiness, Airbnb should create engagement through:

1. Seeing their primary audiences as givers and receivers
Currently most travel exchanges see their customers as guests, as all travel companies do. But what if they saw their audiences as givers and receivers? Suddenly, the nature of the job to get done changes. The value proposition for both receivers and givers centers around the ability to give and receive a good gift. The more gift-giving that occurs, both while the consumer is in the experience and after, the greater the value of the platform to both audiences.

2. Ensuring the journey starts with common cause
When the consumer embraces the common cause, he or she wants to contribute. For Airbnb Local Experiences a key metric of success would be whether or not receivers of the tour embrace the cause suggested by the tour. (This same principle applies to the receivers of the rental). Airbnb should be actively working to create Digital Context around the causes

that start the receiver on a journey. This is the mindset of a company that understands altruistic engagement.

3. Supporting a platform that facilitates gift-giving encounters
Each company's key resource is a smart platform that facilitates encounters between its two primary audiences, guests and home owners. Facilitated encounters are strengthened when they allow for:

- Personal preparation. We've seen how the current Airbnb platform supports the personal preparation of the tour guide in its Experiences feature. They can add personal information about themselves. Receivers of the tour should also be able to do more than just recommend the tour

- Reconnection and reciprocity. That platform for travel should make it easier for individuals to provide in-the-moment feedback, especially about things they like. For example, if a receiver is impressed by the décor when she first enters the home, make it possible for her to quickly say so

- Queuing. The platform should alert consumers in timely ways with recommendations for good gifts while they travel. Why not encourage thoughtfulness on the part of the traveler toward family, hosts, or other travelers while in a rented vacation location

All of these recommendations will help Airbnb move from being a platform for local activities to a platform for friendships and meaningful experience. Those experiences are likely to lead to rebookings and ongoing relationships with customers.

A Perceptive Happiness Engagement Model

There is a certain type of pleasure that comes from sensory experiences that cause you to reflect. Epicurus talked about the joy of food and the meaning associated with the pleasures of life. Companies that produce movies, video, articles, and commercials almost always deliver perceptive happiness (although the content sometimes promises transformation). Perceptive happiness is delivered when an experience regularly creates content that causes the individual to reflect positively and then delivers new content that causes the individual to enjoy the experience again. Pandora is a perceptive happiness engine. You will remember that when it first launched, people were very impressed with its ability to string together related songs. Pandora puts the Music Genome Project into consumers' hands—and by so doing delivers perceptive happiness. To deliver you must excel at:

Perceptive

1. Creating compelling stimulus (sights, sounds, tastes, smells, textures, and so on)

2. Getting people to reflect, slow down, focus, and savor

3. Creating a pattern for newness and adaptation that builds upon previous positive experiences

Digital Context is exciting to advertisers because it suggests the potential for placing the right message in the right place at the right time with greater accuracy. Platforms like HeyStaks (www.heystaks.com) already promise to place the right ad in front of the right consumer through analytics that target consumer context and interests. HeyStaks calls profiling customers' interests and context for advertising, "intent-oriented segmentation." The company asserts that "Creating an audience segment defined by topic-based preferences means exactly the right target users can be included, without including large numbers of people for whom a campaign will hold little relevance. A user's interests and context define their current intent, so these segments contain the users with a high probability of converting."

While the platform sounds very promising for advertisers and search-based ad platforms, one wonders what the impact of this approach would be on a home or car owner with many connected devices. Would every moment become a sales moment? How painful! The closer that advertising comes to the point of use, the more the purpose of messaging must change. Content, whether generated for consumption or persuasion, must support the moment and the mode.

In the Digital Consumer Collaborative's research we explored the question: What does it take to get a consumer to switch modes? The answer: very little. And you can imagine the impact of a targeted campaigned aimed at getting consumers to buy every time they are in a mode. It would frustrate people and make them want to turn the product off. However, the exact same technology employed to produce Perceptive Happiness could enhance the happiness of consumers, improve their wellbeing, build trust, and weave content into the fabric of life.

Let's use a platform like HeyStak to deliver on Perceptive Happiness through Digital Context. We have at our disposal an analytics tool that tracks consumer activity, has permission to use location, social, tool productivity, and brand data to serve up content that causes consumers to reflect positively. The current platform uses key words and domain names to derive interest. But our tool will also target modes. HeyStak's new business model focuses on helping brands to create meaningful content moments for consumers in environments and across tools or platforms. In our scenario, retailers hire HeyStak's intent-based methodology to help them deliver meaningful reflective experiences on an ongoing basis. How does it work?

Step 1. HeyStak decides to partner with media content providers to produce the Package. This is a key activity for both the data analytics company and the media company. Perceptive engagement is built on content—and data about how the consumer responds to that content. The Package should delight the consumer each time the consumer receives new content. By monitoring user activity in different environments, HeyStak creates, on the fly, content requirements for the consumer's situation. It's the content provider's job to ensure content that fits the situation is ready.

Step 2. Through queues and tools, content becomes 'readied' for the consumer. We are used to opening our Facebook tool and seeing social postings of friends. With Digital Context, we should be able to open Facebook and see postings that pertain to where we are, what we are doing, and the mode that we are in. Getting ready to start dinner? Imagine that all of your tools respond to provide helpful content as you prepare for dinner. But they don't force it on you. You know that you can access the content by bringing up the right queue.

Step 3. HeyStak and the Media company use the insights from usage to understand new patterns of emotional engagement and to support emotional jobs that customers have while in key modes. Done right, this learning platform, will develop trust while improving the wellbeing of the individual. Is it then okay to advertise occasionally? Sure, but the content of the advertising should support the positive patterns that have been created, not block them.

Advertising can produce meaningful experiences. The goal of this type of campaign is not to measure number of eyeballs. Instead, it focuses on measuring trust. Does the consumer trust the brands more and give more permission for data sharing? How does that trust manifest itself in ongoing relationships with the brand? These are the types of things we need to focus on.

A Utilitarian Happiness Engagement Model

Utilitarian Happiness doesn't concern itself with *eudaimonia* or as they say in positive psychology, "flourishing." The other three types of happiness encourage reflection, goal attainment, and sharing. Utilitarian happiness? Not so much. The goal of this type of happiness is maximized pleasure. If Perceptive happiness is emotional; Transformative happiness is aspirational; and Altruistic happiness is social; then Utilitarian is plain ol' functional happiness. Sometimes, we just want the most sensory activity in the highest quantities in the least amount of time. And typically we want that roller coaster ride to be provided by others while we play a passive, participative role.

Google Search delivers Utilitarian Happiness. Frito Lay corn chips deliver the same thing. And most war-based games where you shoot as many enemies as you can are, as you can imagine, focused on the utility of pleasure—not some form of flourishing. Diana, one of the participants in our studies, spoke glowingly about her technology because the tools were so powerful, which in turn made her feel very productive. She wrote:

> *"Technology not only supports my modes/moods, it is instrumental. For example, I just recently became a tablet owner (yes, I'm very late) and I have found myself to be incredibly productive ever since (using productivity content such as Evernote, Numbers, Pages, Keynote, etc.). As far as technology supporting my happy mood... social media, movies, music, being able to watch a hockey game on my phone when I'm not at home! Are you kidding me? Technology is key to my happiness."*

For most of us, our digital tools deliver far more capability than we use. But we do use those tools to pack more pleasurable moments into a shorter period of time. Positive Utilitarian engagement can be delivered when the following three things are present:

Utilitarian

1. Powerful tool or environments. The ability of the tool or environment to empower the individual

2. Dramatic action. A rising sense of anticipation and a climatic sensation

3. Newness/adaptation. New experiences that regularly upgrade the previous experience

When these three elements are present, you get fun stuff. It's easy to see how many companies who provide 'dumb' goods, services, or experiences to consumers today are likely to be able to tap into Utilitarian engagement. Products that work together to help consumers get things done can make a big difference.

My colleagues, Martie Woods and Jaclyn DuPont, recently had the opportunity to work with one of the biggest Internet of Things brands in the world. We had been hired by the company to facilitate innovative employee development programming in Barcelona. The events were to be hosted there because the company had been instrumental in helping the city become a 'smart city.' Much of what technology does to improve the lives of residents in a smart city involves powerful tools that speed up activities that would otherwise be characterized by delay, congestion, or tedium. But as Lesson Six stipulates, in addition to speeding up activities, such smart technology must also improve the residents' well-being.

Barcelona has implemented a number of new technologies to make the city smarter. They include sensors in the local parks that manage the irrigation of lawns and gardens as well as sending data to gardening crews; a network of buses that drive their routes based on analyses of common congestion and traffic patterns; garbage cans that can sense when cans are full; and traffic light systems that respond to emergency service vehicle routes, allowing the vehicles to arrive faster.

This kind of integration of technologies into an environment, like a city, improves individual lives as well as the general quality of life for people living in the city. Whether at home, in the car, at the store, or on vacation, consumers are likely to benefit from the integration of smart technologies, purely for functional reasons.

Corning created Gorilla Glass, a lightweight optical glass that is currently used in billions of smart phones. It's touch sensitive. They also produce Elevecture, a smart glass wall technology. Corning has the ability to outfit your kitchen with wall to wall screens. Your kitchen island could be an end-to-end touch screen. (And yes, you could still dice vegetables on it). Let's imagine a Utilitarian engagement model in a home where the entire kitchen is a smart surface.

The goal of Utilitarian engagement is to maximize the pleasure from a staged experience through powerful tools, dramatic action, and newness and adaptation. We know from our research that consumers value being able to maximize their 'total volume of attention.' So, we are going to design an experience where a mother who is cooking dinner for her family can also catch up on her social networks, search for places to plan her family vacations, and otherwise do whatever it is she wants to in the moment.

Step 1. We begin by providing environmental support for a range of relaxing or productivity modes. Consumers use powerful tools to help them be more productive and also to help them relax. So we target key modes that are aligned with both sides of the spectrum and expand the experience within the kitchen. The more modes we support, the more options available to our consumer. Remember that she can be cooking *while* she's planning a family vacation. So don't limit her to just one mode. We give her space on our kitchen island to do both.

Step 2. Next we anticipate and automate tasks she really doesn't need or want to do. Part of what makes her feel empowered is when things are at her beck and call. On the surface, queue up the next steps she's likely to want to take. A touch, a word, or gesture from her will signal whether she agrees with what you've suggested. Orchestrate across activities so that the activity she is most likely to want to do next is close by. The greater the orchestration between tools, the more likely you are to surprise and delight her.

Step 3. We use previous experiences and curated recommendations to improve her experience the next time. While she may not be planning her vacation next time, she will likely have other activities she wants to do while she cooks. Use knowledge of her schedule to make suggestions. If we are providing the algorithm of a dinner recipe and we know that in the past she has wanted to use less salt than called for, suggest that.

This type of an environment becomes the field of play for other products and services who are seeking her attention. Or in other words, other products and services can engage with consumers through your platform. It's your job to manage that field of play. Data gathered from the use of powerful tools and high performance environments benefits adjacent goods, services, and experiences. You've created prime decision-making real estate and your data can help other products to improve. That's why revenue sharing agreements with partners are likely to be one source of funding.

By focusing on maximum benefit with minimum effort, you develop value propositions that create powerful benefits to your customer. She will value the journey in part because of the 'rush' or feeling of dramatic action that comes from operating seamlessly in concert with her kitchen environment.

Each Model Creates Positive Engagement

Each model described creates positive engagement. Each model improves the wellbeing of the consumer in a different way. None of the models are based on a loyalty program. I imagine that every company that focuses on positive engagement will find variations on the four approaches above. The important thing is that you understand what are the things that actually produce happiness and become successful at those things. Remember, I'm not talking about promising happiness. That's easy. I mean, you must deliver experiences that include the elements described above.

The next time you are in an ideation session, try using the four archetypes to brainstorm new approaches to product design, marketing strategy, customer service, or customer journey. They work. They take you down different paths than you would normally go. And if you are designing your company's digital strategy, think big. Think wellbeing. Imagine the positive impact you can have if you do things right.

CHAPTER SEVEN

DOING DIGITAL STRATEGY: A CONCEPT CASE STUDY

Applying Digital Context lessons to
Procter & Gamble's Swiffer Wet Jet Mop

Lesson 7: Doing Digital Strategy: A Concept Case Study

Let's take the lessons from each of the six chapters and apply them to a specific situation. In this fictional case study, I'm going to use a common product, P&G's Swiffer, to show how a company might go about creating a strategy to engage consumers and leverage Digital Context.

Why This Fictional Case Study?

I can already hear that skeptical executive in your organization saying, "See, I told you, he's not talking about our industry. He's talking about consumer goods. We are different." Some executives will be quick to dismiss Digital Context as something that only pertains to others. I have been a vice president in a brand experience agency and principal of my own consulting group for twenty years. I know that the first thing that runs through an executive's mind upon seeing in a pitch presentation a case study that's not from his or her specific industry. "These guys don't know us. They can't help." There may be some legitimate reasons to have that kind of a response, but oftentimes I think that such a response at minimum limits an organization's ability to learn.

Here are the reasons I chose to use the Swiffer as a fictional concept case study. First, it's a product that was designed to get a job done. Clayton

Christensen, the Harvard professor who popularized jobs to get done, and his consulting group worked with P&G to help create the value proposition for Swiffer. According to their write up, they abandoned the traditional corporate segmentation strategy, which focuses heavily on demographics and psychographics, to create a segmentation approach based on the job rather than the demographic. The Swiffer was a wildly successful innovation for P&G and is often used as an example of what can be accomplished when a company focuses on jobs to get done.

The second reason I chose this product is because it's a very good, dumb tool many people use at home all the time. The home is the hub of so much activity that is increasingly being digitized. Cleaning a home is an interesting activity to think about digitizing. And the third reason I chose this product is because we did *not* study it and we are not working with P&G to design a data experience for the Swiffer. In the Collaborative we have retailers, travel companies, banks, insurance companies, media, agencies, and purveyors of gifts. Stone Mantel has done research for each of these companies in their categories. And while P&G was a client years ago, we don't currently work with them and have never been engaged in developing strategy for Swiffer. So, this is a bit of a free gift to them and a way of not discussing other activities that might impinge on members of the Collaborative.

As we go through this fictional case study, which again is not based on anything that P&G may or may not being doing at the moment, you will need to ask yourself questions about your own organization to draw your own analogies, but the principles should be the same. For this case study I am going to use the principles of design thinking and apply them to Digital Context. I am going to treat data as a strategic resource that should be designed and managed—not just collected and analyzed.

Data Experience Design

If data is a resource that can produce a better experience for consumers and value for companies, then we must evolve the culture of the data analytic types in our companies. Data analytics is dominated by those that can optimize an existing analytics maturity curve, audit a data ecosystem, and use the best instruments to construct and visualize the conversations that occur across the world. Data analysts are continually talking about the potential uses of data; but they struggle to create new solutions that accomplish big things.

> In order to create meaningful, or even disruptive, innovation through data, companies must employ the best practices in design thinking on data.

In order to create meaningful, or even disruptive, innovation through data, companies must employ the best practices in design thinking on data. Stone Mantel has a five-phase design thinking methodology we call the Mantel Method. To design experiences—and we have designed everything from cruise ship milieus to banking products—we Assess, Discover, Define, Demonstrate, and Act. By combining the principles I've shared on Digital Context with the Mantel Method, we can produce data experiences. That is, we can use data to improve the experiences that consumers have with us *and* we can design data to do the things we need it to do. The current focus by the data analytics industry on instrumentation visualizes a lot of random things that are out there but it does not give guidance on the types of data we should be employing to produce new, compelling experiences. So, as we go through this concept case study, I'll point out opportunity areas for Swiffer to use design thinking tied to data that can significantly change the experience.

Now, you might be thinking, "I thought this chapter was on doing digital strategy not data strategy." I'll explain why the two are closely aligned. There is an underlying argument to this book that you have probably picked up on. The design of Digital Context depends upon the sharing and design of data. Data design is as important to companies going forward as app design was for companies first entering the mobile world. Data design is what separates Digital Context from omni-channel strategy. And data design is the 'ask' of the Context Comfortable. Consumers don't want you to collect data on them. They want you to employ data to benefit their wellbeing. So, we gotta get this right. Data design is crucial to digital strategy going forward. And it's all about business strategy.

Swiffer Decides to Be a Smart Tool

Let's imagine that you've been hired as a consultant by P&G to help them design the next generation of Swiffer Wet Jets. P&G understands the potential that including sensors in their products provides but they want to understand how to think holistically about the new solution they are creating. So they've hired you to come in and work with them. It's a good thing that they did because the implications for including sensors in products go well beyond automation. They can affect all parts of a business model.

The first lesson you share with your client is that when it comes to Digital Context, a watch is not a watch. And therefore, a mop is not a mop. Consumers will come to expect more than just a device that cleans up spills. Done properly, this new Wet Jet will connect with other tools within the home to support consumer wellbeing. Consumers should be able to track their cleaning patterns and find ways to improve. They should be able to automate activities they don't want to do – or are prone to forget to do – like purchasing refills of cleaning liquid or wipe pads in a timely fashion. They may also want helpful advice on how to clean different types of floors or handle sticky messes, or how to take advantage of different capabilities of the product itself. And the consumer will want the content to be specific to her situation, not general stuff she could easily look up on Google.

Or is the consumer a he? P&G often defines its target market based first on gender, which makes sense if the decision-maker and user are almost always one gender or the other. But what if the Swiffer could accommodate both men and women? Perhaps men in certain households have a particular way of cleaning floors that differs from women. Could a sensor-driven mopping experience pick up on the differences? How about when children or teenagers use the solution? Or guests? Are there differences in cleaning patterns that matter? These are things that you should examine to determine what new capabilities your context-aware tool should offer. Digital ethnographic research techniques are the best way to explore the potential enhancements that this new solution should deliver. Once you've gathered insights into the additional functional, emotional, social, and aspirational jobs that consumers can and want to do you can begin to articulate a vision of what the solutions potential is for Swiffer and adjacent products.

Of course, you don't want the Swiffer laden with complexity. You still want to create a simple albeit effective experience, but you need to know what the potential opportunity is and you need to be aware of how activity captured by the Swiffer might connect to other activities in your home. So you do your research.

Developing a Marketing Plan

From the fieldwork and other research you conduct you discover that the greatest opportunity for Swiffer is to go after Rapid Cleaning mode first and then other modes and jobs to get done. Rapid Cleaning mode is one that both men and women get into on regular basis. And a context-aware Swiffer has the ability to improve the experience dramatically. (Remember, I'm conceptualizing here. I don't know for certain if this mode is what a real Swiffer experience should be built around).

Knowing the modes that matter most to consumers is critical to your ability to help P&G. It's a key lynch pin in your ability to segment your target audience, design a customer journey, and develop a value proposition. Other things change in a marketing plan for a context-aware product. They include:

How A Marketing Plan Changes for Digital Context	
Target Market	Focus on people who are in a target mode doing a recurring job that is part of your value proposition.
Goals	Sales, awareness, consideration and engagement are all driven by a company's ability to get into the intimate circle that queueing creates. Set goals for wellbeing and usage in your field of play by your target market.
Brand Strategy	Positive engagement means that your positioning should be purpose driven. Promise keeping requires a commitment to activities that increase trust.
Emerging Opportunities	APIs & SDKs matter in Digital Context. Your best opportunities will come from increased ability to leverage data. Look for recurring jobs to do. Be the connector.
Marketing Mix	Track the evolution of your channels. The more smart channels there are, the more the Package matters to you.

To help P&G develop its marketing plan for Swiffer, you focus on five important steps. They are:

1. Define or segment your target market by modes

2. Revise your value proposition and address the functional, emotional, social, and aspirational jobs to get done

3. Set goals for wellbeing and field of play usage

4. Map and design a customer journey that addresses modes, milestones, queues and context

5. Work to create an engagement strategy that maximizes happiness and increases profitability

Modes, Segments, Journeys, and Value Propositions for Swiffer

In this scenario, let's say that you sit down with the brand leader for Swiffer, her team and her agencies, and together you define the strategy. Karen is the brand leader and she starts off the conversation, which goes something like this:

> Karen: Our prime target has always been women between the ages of 32 and 45 who have an average household income of $95k, are college educated, with three kids and a career. We call our prime customer, Sara.
>
> (If Clayton Christensen's team is right then this is *not* how the conversation would start because the Swiffer team segments based on jobs to get done, rather than demographics. Nevertheless, most companies don't. So please allow me a little bit of creative license here).
>
> You: Right, and now we want to think about your prime target differently. Instead of defining your target audience based on 'who' she is, I'm asking you to define your target audience based on a mode that Sara and Sara's husband have in common. They both understand and get into Rapid Cleaning mode.
>
> Karen: Okay, and you've done ethnographic and quant and can tell me things like the importance of this 'mode', the size of the opportunity, and the patterns associated with the mode?
>
> You: We have. And I can tell you that if you focus on Rapid Cleaning you can both narrow your target and broaden your reach. You can go after a very specific situation while addressing a much wider audience than Sara.
>
> At this point you show her this slide.

1. DEFINING A TARGET MARKET

Shifting the target focus from a 'who' to a 'mode' helps Swiffer to broaden its reach *and* narrow its target: wider audience/specific situation.

Swiffer Traditional Prime Target Persona

Sara is a working mother of three. She wants to spend less time cleaning her house and more time creating meaningful experiences for her family.

Demographics
32- 45 years old
$95,000 combined income
College educated

Interests
Family sporting activities
A clean house

Mode Prime Target

People who are in Rapid Cleaning Mode.

Circumstances/Scenario
Family/Weeknight
When working families come home to have dinner together the frequency of spills. Families, and mothers in particular, go into Rapid Cleaning mode.

Individual
When individuals want to clean their hardwood floors as efficiently as they can, they go into Rapid Cleaning mode.

You: You see, we want to define your target market in terms of Rapid Cleaning mode, which is a big shift from the way you've traditionally approached things.

Karen: So help me. What do we gain by defining our target market this way?

Karen's question is important. And you have a list at the ready. They include the following:

- Modes align with consumer attitudes and behavior today

- Modes support Digital Context

- By focusing on them, you target moments rather than demographics

- They help you keep your focus on what you need to accomplish for consumers

- Consumers will give you permission to know what mode they are in

- You can design data experiences to support modes

- They allow you to keep all of the customers you currently have without alienating any customer who is in the mode at any given time

- It is easier to keep your promises and deliver meaningful experiences

And so Karen decides to move forward. Now, based on her decision you can begin to talk about customer journey and value proposition very differently than before. First let's take a look at customer journey. Rapid Cleaning is clearly not the only mode that consumers go into. They have full lives. They have multiple things going on at the same time. As you begin to explore how highly connected home and family dynamics unfold for consumers, your map of a typical household might look like the following:

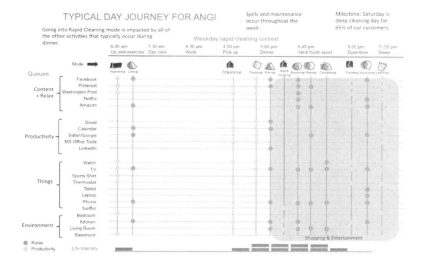

Again, I've created this solely for the purposes of illustrating an approach to customer journey. It combines insights from a real life consumer, Angi, with examples of tools and environments that are connected to the typical consumer's life. Notice that this map shows that her experience is supported by queues that she engages with on a regular basis. Sometimes she engages with these queues to relax and sometimes she engages with them to be more productive. This journey map shows how Rapid Cleaning fits within the life of the consumer. By extrapolating insights from field work, surveys, and data collected from consumers, you can begin to see high potential moments—even if very short—when Rapid Cleaning is likely to happen; although who can ever time when a spill will happen? You can also begin to see the relationship between modes, queues, tools, and environments. These relationships present opportunities to deepen connections. And although your first iterations of a sensor driven Swiffer experience probably won't tap into other modes, queues, or tools, knowing those relationship potentials will help you design the type of data you need to collect and employ.

There are likely other ways to view the customer journey that emphasize the mode over a linear, monolithic framework, but your client gets the idea. She sees the potential for viewing at least the usage part of the journey through the lens of modes and queues. Your conversation continues and others begin to chime in.

The advertising agency representative's main concern centers on product positioning. He or she wants to know, based on what the team already knows about the dynamics of the home environment, what your goals for Swiffer going forward should be. In other words, what are some of the positive things that can be accomplished to benefit the home and the consumer and deepen the relationship between consumer and the company?

It's the right question to ask, and the answer to it requires the rest of the team to become involved with developing the strategy. For example, Research & Development knows that its sensors can connect with a home environment system like Google Nest, they can provide data about usage, refill frequency, and can connect to other P&G cleaning brands like Mr. Clean. That kind of data provides the ability to show people how cleaning floors fits into their lives, how much time they spend cleaning their home, and even when they are most likely to experience a spill. It also enables the company to make their customers feel good about their homes, and about the effectiveness of the cleaning solutions it provides.

The marketing staff knows essentially that it has permission to gather tool productivity data, brand data, and environmental control data, but does not have permission from consumers to tap into social, location, or, importantly, queue data. From marketing's perspective, thought may need to be given to the question of whether or not the company should go after permission to collect these data types or stay focused on delivering an experience based on the permissions the company already has.

Much of this boils down to a key question: how do you positively engage consumers and support Rapid Cleaning mode?

Again, a good question. But before you can answer it, you need articulate a value proposition. What is it exactly that you are offering? The group decides to step back for a moment and focus on the value proposition for a context-aware Swiffer. A mode-based value proposition focuses on the mode, the recurring job to get done, and the solution. To illustrate the difference from the traditional value proposition, you show the group this slide:

2. REVISE YOUR VALUE PROPOSITION   **Version 1**

Focus on people who are in a target mode doing a recurring job that is part of your value proposition.

Traditional Value Proposition

Customer: Our best customers are women between the ages of 26 and 45.

Problem: Who do not have time to mop their hardwood floors.

Solution: The Swiffer Wet Jet offers an all-on-one mop starter kit with magic strips and a flexible head.

Based on Vlaskovits & Cooper's CPS technique
Customer: _____ (who your customer is).
Problem: _____ (what problem you're solving for the customer).
Solution: _____ (what is your solution for the problem).

Mode Value Proposition

Mode: Rapid Cleaning. When people are pressed for time and want to clean up.

Job: People hire tools that clean floors with minimal effort that makes them feel powerful and in control.

Recurrence: Each time they clean they like to having disposable floor wipes and replenished liquid cleaner.

Solution: The Swiffer Wet Jet offers an all-on-one mop starter kit with magic strips and a flexible head. When the packet of magic strips runs out a button lights up that when pressed reorders more strips.

___ Functional and emotional jobs

Karen (she's our brand leader) notes that despite the fact that there are any number of things that you *could* do, by 1) focusing the value proposition on a key mode (and, yes there could be multiple modes), 2) reminding your team why the consumer hires the tool—in this case to clean floors and make them feel in control—and then 3) focusing on what makes the job a recurring job that consumers value, the value proposition helps the team to stay focused on what should be promised and what should be delivered.

A Positive Engagement Strategy

The discussions among the team that have led up to the value proposition reminded the group that the more the new Swiffer can do the more important it is that the company ensure the actual experience lives up to the promise. The Swiffer must deliver a better Rapid Cleaning experience before it can become a trusted part of the Digital Context home. The team wants to deliver an experience that improves the wellbeing of the user. You recommend that the team adopt a positive engagement strategy based on Utilitarian happiness. You remind the team that, of the four types of happiness (Transformative, Altruistic, Perceptive, and Utilitarian), Utilitarian fits this product the best. Utilitarian happiness comes from powerful tools that build dramatic action and are upgraded or adapted over time to keep things new.

As a group you decide to write a commitment to positive engagement statement that will guide the team's strategy and design activities. The positive engagement statement reads:

Our commitment to positive engagement

1. We promise to create Rapid Cleaning mode tools that have the most helpful disposable cleaning strips and momentized floor cleaning tips.

We keep that promise through regular innovation and improvement to our cleaning strips and by developing a content platform that provides customized tips every Saturday to consumers who subscribe. All content is provided to the consumer through their queue of choice.

2. We promise to use data collected from the Swiffer, the home environment, and from other P&G brands to positively impact the customer's experience.

We keep that promise by focusing data analytics on how to maximize an individual's productivity during Rapid Cleaning mode to ensure that the consumer feels in control and finishes with minimal effort. We use the data to support replenishment of supplies and to recommend upgrades. We share data with other P&G brands that support similar modes.

The first promise you make will help improve customer happiness by focusing data design on producing a more powerful tool. The second promise will deliver customer happiness by regularly surprising and delighting consumers with ideas on how to improve their productivity.

Your commitment to the consumer implies that you will be offering recommendations to consumers. You will be using their data combined with your content to create a very personalized set of recommendations for the consumer. That's the Package. So you recommend that you addend the Swiffer positive engagement promise with a statement on the Package. It reads:

How We Design the Package
As solution providers we design content that is delivered to customer queues that supports them before, during, and after first use, according to household cleaning patterns, and at the time of refill. The Package design supports the multiple modes that our customers are in.

How The Package works:

Content
- Surprises
- Tips & Advice
- Alerts
- Packaging

- Offers

Data
- Time of day
- Time of week
- Frequency of use
- Length of use
- Purchase date
- Other P&G brands

Data shared about consumer activity is used to identify the right content at the right time.

- Purchase
- Reuse
- Replace

Your goal in designing the Package is to create an experience that surprises and delights the consumer. Timing is everything. Design is so important. While these documents look really good to the group, the proof is in the pudding. So using your drafted value proposition, customer journey, and positive engagement statement as guidelines, Karen asks the team to develop concepts and prototypes to share with customers. Using co-creation techniques, you study the concepts and find ways to improve. At the end of this phase, you rewrite your value proposition, your journey strategy, and your positive engagement statement to reflect your new understanding of what the consumer in Rapid Cleaning mode is looking for. Here's what a rewritten value proposition might look like:

2. REVISE YOUR VALUE PROPOSITION   **Final Version**
Co-create with your target audience your value proposition.

Swiffer Context-Aware Wet Jet Value Proposition   *Positive engagement through Utilitarian Happiness*

Mode	Jobs	Job Recurrence
Rapid Cleaning. When people have another pressing activity but need to stop and clean the floors before they can do anything else.	Functional: People hire tools that clean floors with minimal effort. Emotional: They want to feel powerful and in control. Aspirational: Improve overall household cleanliness throughout the week. And improve the wellbeing of members of the home.	1. Each time the Swiffer is used, the tool logs, time of day, time of week, frequency of use, length of use, replenishment/purchase date, and data from other P&G brands. Data is used to support content that regularly shows up in queues with advice and logs on cleaning activity.
Getting into Rapid Cleaning mode means • Stopping everything else • Focus on floors • Focus also on table/counter top • Be thorough • Keep conversation going.		2. Before they run out people like to having disposable floor wipes and replenished liquid cleaner.

Solution: The Swiffer Context-Aware Wet Jet Solution combines an all-on-one mop starter kit with magic strips and a flexible head with data experiences that help households clean faster, smarter, and more thoroughly. The solution improves the wellbeing of members of the household through personalized advice, logs, and support for other cleaning activities.

Evolving to New Modes and Models of Engagement

Now, let's imagine that the new context-aware Swiffer has been out on the market for a good period of time. Sales have been very good. The company is pleased and ready to start thinking about the next phases in developing solutions for Swiffer. You've been called back in to help the organization think about evolving to new modes and models of engagement. You outline a five-step plan for the company to follow. The steps are:

1. Identify jobs in queues and modes related to the tools you presently provide or might provide going forward.

2. Create or partner with solutions that support related jobs.

3. Create metrics for wellbeing based on engagement and key emotional, social, and aspirational jobs.

4. Evolve your business model.

5. Evolve your engagement model.

Step 1: Identify jobs in queues and modes related to the tools you presently provide or might provide going forward.
One of the first exercises you have Karen's team do is to gather together all of the research you have collected on the jobs consumers are trying to get

done with Swiffer. To help you facilitate a discussion about the opportunities and gaps in your understanding of the jobs to get done, you create a worksheet that looks something like this:

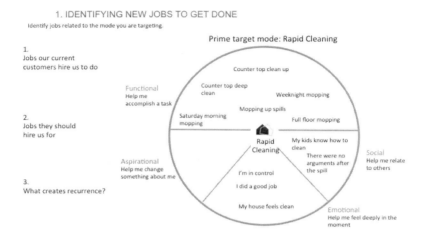

Team members are asked to think about three things: what are the jobs customers currently hire Swiffer to do? What are the jobs they should hire us to do? And what about these jobs creates recurrence. You plot the types of jobs that consumers want to get done, paying attention to functional, emotional, social, and aspirational jobs. The jobs are mapped based on their proximity to Rapid Cleaning mode.

Using the group's work as a starting point, you encourage the team to vet the map. The team has data collected from Swiffer, access to consumer panels, and the ability to do in-home observation work. The more you learn, the more dimensionalized the map becomes and the more confident you become about new jobs and new modes to go after.

Step 2: Create or partner with solutions that support related jobs.
Once you've identified new jobs and modes to go after, the question becomes how to support those jobs. Sure, you could continue to create new versions of Swiffer apps and tools to narrowly support these known jobs. But, you might want to look around and see what other products are within your

field of play that can help you accomplish more. In P&G's case they have a veritable arsenal of cleaning brands that could benefit from a coordinated effort to support consumer modes. Karen recognizes this and she suggests you consider as a part of your strategy how Mr. Clean and Bounty can fit into your strategic approach. You prepare a table for Karen that shows how Mr. Clean, Bounty, and Swiffer can partner together to support cleaning solutions within the home. The table includes the following:

	Mr. Clean	**Swiffer**	**Bounty**
Jobs related to Rapid Cleaning	Decontaminate dirty areas	Mop up spills	Wipe down dirty areas fast
What data is shared by consumers?	Time of day, amount used, frequency of use.	Time of day, time of week, frequency of use, length of use, purchase date.	Refill
What can we do to support Rapid Cleaning?	Provide in queue tips on decontaminating areas.	Provide in queue recommendations for how to reduce clean up time.	Ship Bounty or Swiffer cleaning solutions with refill of Bounty.
How do we strengthen the field of play?	Integrate with other household items.	Share cleaning pattern data with consumer through a life log tool.	To gain more data and eliminate dark spots: provide smart dowel for dispensing sheets.

The table includes recommendations for creating context-aware tools that support the wiping up of other types of spills or household messes. Working together, Mr. Clean data, Swiffer data, and Bounty data can tell both the consumer and P&G a lot about the patterns of activity within the individual home. You must insure that privacy and security are maintained. You must also demonstrate to the consumer that a coordinated set of efforts among smart tools brings a real benefit to the consumer.

3. Create metrics for wellbeing based on engagement and key emotional, social, and aspirational jobs.

As a part of this new coordinated effort among P&G tools, there needs to be some coordination regarding how effective you are at delivering wellbeing to the consumer. All of the products currently deliver Utilitarian benefits. So Karen recommends that all of the brands adopt the same metrics for positive engagement. She proposes to her colleagues that they measure the following things:

- How effective is the tool for Rapid Mode
- What kinds of surprise and delight does the Rapid Clean engagement model create
- What makes the household members feel more in control
- What makes the household members feel like they've done a good job
- What makes the household members feel like the house is clean

The first two metrics are designed to help each brand measure its effectiveness in delivering Utilitarian happiness (powerful tools + surprise and delight). The three additional metrics focus on key emotional jobs you want the new set of solutions to support. If you do a good job with all of these metrics, there's a high likelihood that consumers will continue to engage the solutions. If you don't deliver on these metrics, they will most likely just turn you off.

4. Evolve your business model

The Swiffer team has committed itself to positive engagement. Up till now, the model that has worked is based on Utilitarian happiness, but now with a more holistic set of activities—from wipes to floor mopping—the new set of solutions may just be in the right place to improve other aspects of consumer wellbeing. And with that new set of opportunities comes even more focus on how to develop a new business model that includes smart tools but delivers holistic cleaning support. The data that is generated from consumer activity has become a key resource for the company. The team recognizes that things have gone well and now it is time to become a digital brand that supports cleaning modes.

Karen assembles the team and invites you to facilitate a discussion about what it would mean to shift the business model and become the digital brand that supports a range of cleaning modes.

> You: As more and more products connect to P&G to better support Rapid Cleaning mode or related modes, Swiffer needs to become a multi-sided platform for activity that occurs within the home. The platform's growth means that other more general modes like Planning and Sharing need to be supported. By doing so, P&G can own the field of play for most household cleaning jobs to get done.

> Karen: Okay, show me what that looks like.

> You: I'm suggesting that we start treating Swiffer as a multi-sided business platform. We work to position Swiffer to take on the role of in-home platform provider. The platform becomes a hub for data obtained from goods and services the household uses. Other companies that are also focused on the modes we support and would benefit from the Platform's smarts regarding planning and tracking cleaning activity become a key customer segment for Swiffer.

> Karen: So we now have two target customers: households and other companies who want to deliver home cleaning solutions?

> You: Right, however there is a key difference between your platform and a platform like Facebook and Google Search. Their models rely on advertising to deliver the experience to consumers for free. We know that your customer does not want advertising at the point of use. Instead, we recommend you create a multisided platform that focuses on refills/replenishment. When companies sign up with the Swiffer platform they get data that will help them improve their product and

support the consumer experience. They also participate in a one-step refill/replenishment program.

Karen: So our platform will manage refills/replenishment for other companies? Why wouldn't they simply do that themselves.

You: Because they don't have the consumer trust and engagement that you've built. Consumers rely on the content you provide in their queues. In fact, your app for cleaning activity has become its own queue. From the research I've assembled, it looks like you have as much of their trust as Amazon does. In fact, you have more permission to access more data than they do. And they know it.

You then share with Karen three important paradigm shift statements that better explain the model.

The Key Resource

A network of connected products all focused on helping the household when in cleaning mode becomes more important to the household than the Swiffer mopping system by itself. This is the Swiffer Platform.

The Key Activity

The Key Activities that the Swiffer Platform supports are all cleaning modes and Planning and Sharing modes. Swiffer works to own the field of play for most household cleaning jobs.

Partnerships

P&G actively seeks out partnerships with companies who provide tools that support the platform and strengthen and enlarge the field of play that P&G owns.

Let's Pause to Think

Let me pause in our fictional case study for a second to point out a few things that are likely to happen as companies embrace Digital Context. For some readers, this world that I am trying to create a picture of is starting to get a bit crazy. Suddenly the manufacturer of a mopping system is creating a platform that competes with Amazon for refill business? Is that what your saying, Dave? Are you nuts? I'll answer the first question and let you ponder the second.

Once consumers begin to trust manufacturers, service providers, experience stagers, or anyone else with data about the modes they are in; once consumers give permission to these companies to gather data about location, relationships, environments, brands, and so on, the purpose of the original purchase shifts dramatically. They expect more. And you can deliver more. Your organization needs to think much more expansively about what Digital Context means for you.

P&G is in a pretty good position to own the shelves and floors of the homes that purchase its products. The company should be thinking about how sensor-driven manufactured goods will change the way people think, act, and buy. They should use their advantages to create new advantages for them and the companies that support their goals. On the other hand, Amazon has similar goals. And other brick and mortar retailers have similar goals. We can expect a period of time where, like the VCR/Betamax wars of the 70s, companies vie to become the standard for context-aware solutions. What should be obvious is that every company has a chance to win this game. With some foresight, you can leapfrog the mobility/omni-channel mindset and own the field of play for modes that matter to your consumers.

5. Evolve Your Engagement Strategy

Concurrent with your efforts to evolve your key activities, partnerships and resources, you need to evolve your engagement model. In this case, because your brand owns the platform, its engagement model changes from Utilitarian (Tools, Dramatic Action, Newness) to Altruistic. To do so, Swiffer must excel at creating a common cause that household members agree are important, allowing for personal preparation, facilitating encounters between individuals (most likely through its platform), good gift giving, and allowing for reconnection. Remember that Facebook's engagement strategy is based on Altruistic happiness. You are aiming for that kind of a feeling.

This is a big leap for the company. Everyone on Karen's team understands that in order for the brand to deliver on the experience, you need to get the common cause right. As a team you brainstorm, you study, and you conceptualize. After doing your due diligence you determine that keeping the home clean can be a common cause for households that will bind families to each other and products to households. Since each home has its own patterns the cause is specific to the home and not broad. Your platform, and your business model, will need to address household patterns. A cause that is specific to a small group of individuals is more likely to have potential to charge for a subscription than a broad common cause. And so you explore different pricing models and deliverables associated with your new platforms.

Because the engagement model is altruistic, the platform facilitates key customer activities that make home cleaning feel more like a good gift:

- Personal preparation. The platform helps the consumer feel prepared and congratulates when cleaning is finished

- Reconnection and reciprocity. The platform reminds the next cleaner of steps taken by previous cleaner

Additionally, Swiffer must change the metrics it uses to measure customer wellbeing to include questions that support the Altruistic engagement model. Questions might include:

- How prepared did you feel to accomplish cleaning activities today

- How helpful was the Swiffer platform in helping your household feel clean and its members feel connected to each other

- How effective is the Swiffer platform in helping your household believe in the importance of a clean home

It's A Wrap

There are a lot of additional steps that you will probably want to take. Like all innovation projects, you will need research, strategy, concepts, and the ability to pilot. The work we do in the Digital Collaboratives helps the companies who participate to think forward and anticipate the type of strategies they will need to go forward. Hopefully, this book has provoked your thinking and pushed you to pay attention to things that you weren't previously pondering. The seven lessons I've shared are general findings. If you're company is a member of the Digital Collaboratives, you should reach out to Stone Mantel or your colleague who participated to learn more about your company's strategy for Digital Context. If you are not a member of the Digital Collaboratives, consider joining so that you can help your company prepare for its three-year time horizon.

Before I finish, let's cover the seven lessons one more time:

Lesson 1: A Watch is not a Watch
A watch is not a watch. An IoT-enabled razor is not a razor. An IoT-enabled hearing aid is not a hearing aid. They can each do the basic functionality that the name implies but they do much more and will be hired by consumers to do more than what the name of the item suggests. The consumer hires the tool to do much more than what you originally intended the product to do. Any dumb tool or environment that becomes smart and helps to support Digital Context will enable the consumer in ways that help them to think and to act. Digital Context is about empowerment. The more tools that connect to each other the more each tool becomes a part of an ecosystem that supports other activities. That ecosystem will change your business model.

Lesson 2: Over Time All Channels Become Queues

Over time all channels become queues. Critical to every business model are the marketing, transactional, and customer service channels that ensure that you can share your offerings with your customers. We have progressed from a world of single channels, to multi-channels, to omni-channels, and now to Digital Context. Along the way the channel has become smart and when channels become smart they queue things. The implications for all business is dramatic.

Lesson 3: Consumers Get that Context Requires Data

Despite the constant hacks and security breaches, most consumers share their data with companies freely *if they understand and agree to the purpose for sharing the data.* The Internet of Things and Digital Context depend upon the free flow of data between things. In chapter three, we will discuss the reasons why consumers share data, who the Context Comfortables are, and why they are important to every company's business strategy.

Lesson 4: Design Your Value Proposition to Target a Consumer Mode

Increasingly, if companies are to be relevant and differentiated to their customers, they will need to understand modes. Modes are ways of thinking and behaving that consumers 'get into' that helps them get things done. By targeting a mode for your value proposition, you are effectively aligning your goods, services, or experiences with the way that consumers go about doing what they want to do. Traditionally companies have focused their value propositions on target demographics. But in a highly connected world, what could be more powerful than to be known for supporting a mode that essentially transcends a one-dimensional demographic?

Lesson 5: Data + Content Creates the Package

Companies that are focused on creating content for distribution should turn their attention to focusing on ways to create the Package. Smart Media companies need to find ways to increase the amount of data that travels with the content they produce. In Digital Context, consumers will want their content to be informed by different data types. Companies are used to very basic data being embedded in or attached to content. However, context-aware content requires that companies find ways to share data about biometrics, queues, relationships, environments, brands, and other data types.

Lesson 6: Don't Focus on Loyalty; Focus on Positive Engagement
The promise of Digital Context cannot just be to speed things up. Context must improve the wellbeing of people. There is so much research that is currently going on in positive psychology that help companies think about delivering happiness to consumers. Digital Context should tap into that body of research. On the other hand, companies cannot create context without a return on their investment. Their return will come from ongoing, positive engagement with consumers. This chapter explores why a loyalty mindset is wrong for Digital Context and why a positive engagement mindset is what companies need to go after.

Lesson 7: Doing Digital Strategy: A Case Study
We can use the lessons from the other chapters and brings them together to show how a company might produce solutions that support Digital Context. P&G's Swiffer is only one example. There are so many other companies who are on the cusp of new, bigger opportunities to engage with consumers. On behalf of the Digital Consumer Collaborative, I wish them the very best.

To Learn More

If you would like to go deeper around any of the seven lessons or get access to the original research findings, please contact me at davenorton@gostonemantel.com. Or come to our websites: goStoneMantel.com and theDigitalCollaboratives.com.

About Dave Norton

For over twenty years, Dave has led research and strategy work for clients around the world. Dave founded the Digital Collaboratives in 2013 to help companies collaborate in conducting research about consumers and the impact of digital in their lives. Because of his research and thought leadership, he is one of the youngest recipients of Brigham Young University's highest award for honored alumni.

Dave has lectured at Harvard, Columbia Business School and at Fortune magazine's annual summits. He has taught at Brigham Young University, the University of Minnesota, and Minneapolis College of Art and Design. Since 2005, Stone Mantel has guided hundreds of brand experience leaders in creating meaningful brand experiences.

Dave Norton, Ph.D.

Founder and Principal

Stone Mantel & The Digital Collaboratives

davenorton@gostonemantel.com

gostonemantel.com

thecollaboratives.com